Trials and Tribulations

ALSO BY WILLIAM M. KUNSTLER

Our Pleasant Vices
The Law of Accidents
Corporate Tax Summary
First Degree
. . . .And Justice for All
Beyond A Reasonable Doubt?
The Case for Courage
The Minister and the Choir Singer
Deep In My Heart
The Hall-Mills Murder Case

Trials and Tribulations

WILLIAM M. KUNSTLER

Grove Press Inc./ New York

First Hardcover Edition 1985
First Printing 1985
ISBN: 0-394-54611-3
Library of Congress Catalog Card Number: 84-73209

First Evergreen Edition 1985
First Printing 1985
ISBN: 0-394-62060-7
Library of Congress Catalog Card Number: 84-73209

Signed and Limited Edition
First Printing 1985
ISBN: 0-394-54671-7
Library of Congress Catalog Card Number: 84-73209

Library of Congress Cataloging in Publication Data

Kunstler, William Moses, 1919–
    Trials and tribulations.

    1. Sonnets, American. I. Title.
PS3561.U56T7 1985   811'.52   84-73209
ISBN 0-394-54611-3
ISBN 0-394-62060-7 (pbk.)
ISBN 0-394-54671-7 (lim. ed.)

Printed in the United States of America

GROVE PRESS, INC., 196 West Houston Street, New York, N.Y. 10014

1 3 5 4 2

To Margie, Sarah and Emily

Contents

Preface

The 102 sonnets in this volume were, with rare exceptions, all begun during quiet moments in various courtrooms around the country. The first, "Jury Selection," was written in the summer of 1981 in Providence, Rhode Island, during the actual impaneling of a jury that eventually acquitted two defendants accused of murder; and the last one, "Daddy King," just days ago while I was waiting for a sentence reduction hearing to begin in a Newark, New Jersey, federal courthouse. In between, the sonnets first saw the light of day in such other localities as Albany, Kingston, and Poughkeepsie, New York; Rapid City and Custer, South Dakota; Harrisburg and Philadelphia, Pennsylvania; Richmond and Norfolk, Virginia; Oklahoma City, Oklahoma; Boston and New Bedford, Massachusetts; Concord, New Hampshire; Asheville, North Carolina; Hackensack and Paterson, New Jersey; Sebring, Florida; Bismarck, North Dakota; and, of course, my own bailiwick of New York City.

I chose the sonnet form because, like the law, it has a rather rigid and well-defined structure. In addition, its regular meter and rhyming scheme, as well as the utility of the final couplet to summarize or explain the first twelve lines, seemed to fit in with my intent to write political verse. Lastly, through the centuries, it has been the respected standby of many extraordinary English-language poets such as Edmund Spenser, William Shakespeare, Elizabeth Barrett Browning, William Butler Yeats, and Edna St. Vincent Millay, to name a few, and I felt that, if it worked well for them, it just might do the same for me.

The subjects in this collection are, in a sense, legal or pseudolegal ones. Some, like "Jury Selection," and "Expert Witness," relate to my view of the various stages or aspects of the judicial process. Others, such as "Death Penalty" and "The Supreme Court," reflect my personal thoughts on certain of our legal institutions or values. Still others, like "Martin Luther King, Jr.," "Adam Clayton Powell, Jr.," and "Jack Ruby," contain my impressions of some memorable clients whom I have represented during my professional career. There are also a handful dealing with

American foreign policy, particularly in Latin America and the Caribbean.

In such poems as "Cross Examination," I have concerned myself with what I perceive to be prevailing legal mythologies. There are those sonnets that depict historical events or places with which some of my clients have been associated over the years, such as "Attica," "Wounded Knee," "Puerto Rico," and "Kent State." Lastly, there are two which contain my somewhat ambivalent feelings about the late Judge Julius Jennings Hoffman, who presided at the tumultuous Chicago Conspiracy Trial in 1969–70, at the conclusion of which he sentenced me to more than four years in jail for contempt of court—one written before and the other after his death last year.

Under ordinary circumstances, I do not believe that poetry should ever need explanatory comments. However, I also realize that the passage of time may have blurred the memory of some of the relevant events or personalities of the sonnets. Accordingly, I have decided to give enough background so that some of the poems would not have to stand on their own iambic pentameter alone. There is no requirement, of course, that readers look behind any sonnet, but I am sure that there will be some readers who would like to know more about the characters, events, or ideas that led to the sonnets' creation.

I want to thank my patient colleagues—Robert and Mark Gombiner, Ronald L. Kuby, Shaw-Lee Haynes, Sharon Friedman and Gavrielle Gemma—who listened dutifully to most of these sonnets shortly after they were first written, and, on so many occasions, caught mistakes in scanning, inaccuracies in description, and inappropriate words or phrases; Joan L. Washington, who typed and retyped so much of the manuscript; Max Gartenberg, my agent, whose suggestions about format added a new dimension to my efforts; Barney and Lisa Rosset and their helpful staff at Grove Press, who made it possible for this collection to reach an infinitely wider audience than my own circle of friends and coworkers.

Finally, I want to express my deep gratitude to the many clients I have been privileged to represent over the long years, and the lawyers, paralegals, law students, and legal workers who made it possible for me to do so. In that vein I must give a special nod to the Center for Constitutional Rights with which I have been associated since its founding in 1966. Its resources and moral support enabled me to participate in the various cases and causes which inspired most of the sonnets in this volume.

December 1, 1984   WILLIAM M. KUNSTLER

Trials and Tribulations

Jury Selection

In any criminal trial, jury selection is half the battle. Most defense lawyers feel, once the panel is seated, that the die is cast one way or the other. Some forty years ago, however, the federal courts usurped the time-honored right of attorneys to interrogate prospective jurors on their qualifications by giving the trial judge the option of conducting this examination (*voir dire*) to the exclusion of counsel, an invitation that has almost universally been accepted. This example has been followed in a growing number of states, and in New York there have been, in virtually every recent legislative session thus far, narrowly unsuccessful attempts to adopt the federal rule.

The rationale for eliminating lawyers from the *voir dire* process is, generally, that the judge can conduct the questioning in a much shorter amount of time, thus saving the taxpayers a great deal of money. The elevation of expediency over justice, in my opinion, has vitiated the constitutional imperative of an impartial jury since judges, even with the best of intentions, simply cannot know the intimate details of the cases they are trying as well as do defense attorneys and, therefore, do not frame the appropriate queries. In addition, the courts tend to ask stereotypical questions that do not adequately explore such vital areas as racism, prejudice, religious views, and political ideology.

For almost forty years I have been involved in the process of selecting juries throughout the United States. Initially, except in obvious instances of expressed prejudice, I have depended primarily on visceral feelings and intuition in challenging prospective jurors. Recently, however, in highly controversial cases I have utilized the services of the National Jury Project, an organization which employs the assistance of sociologists, body language experts, and others to aid attorneys in choosing jurors. While the ultimate responsibility still rests with trial lawyers, the specialists make the selection process somewhat more rational than the usual gut feeling assessments.

The reference to "Caesar's heirs" relates, of course, to the custom of having the emperor or his surrogate, at the conclusion of gladiators' bouts in the Roman Colosseum, signify by an up-

turned or lowered thumb whether a vanquished fighter was to
live or die.

Jury Selection

They come and go, these ciphers from the list,
    Computerized into the courtroom sphere,
To pause, then vanish back into the mist
    Of where rejected jurors disappear.
As each new candidate pops up in line,
    The lawyers search for some revealing clue—
A smile, a frown, a glance, or other sign—
    That might divulge a pertinent point of view.
Then come the endless questions, fast or slow,
    From total strangers dressed in somber tones,
Designed to liberate the hidden flow
    Of random thoughts that lie beneath the bones.
At last the box is filled with Caesar's heirs
    Who flex their thumbs and sink into their chairs.

The Supreme Court

The Supreme Court's perceptible drift toward antilibertarianism, particularly since the seating of Sandra Day O'Connor, Reagan's only appointee, recently prompted one of its members to comment publicly that it "condoned both isolated and systematic violations of civil liberties." Another member added that the Court was "moving to the right," and going "where it wants to go . . . by hook or by crook." In area after area—those of affirmative action, access to the federal courts criminal law, capital punishment, church and state, women's rights, national security, freedom of information, antitrust and labor relations—the Burger Court has begun to roll back the clock as fast and as comprehensively as it can and often at the expense of both law and logic. Where necessary, it has bent precedent in ways that would have shocked and dismayed Chief Justice John Marshall, the pioneer who carved out its basic right of review—not to speak of those who drafted the guarantees of individual rights and liberties in Philadelphia in 1787.

The Supreme Court

Each day, precisely at the stroke of ten,
    They stream, in hierarchical array,
Into their seats, one woman and eight men,
    To listen to the cases of the day.
For some the Constitution is as dead
    As those who once spelled out its terms,
For others still there is no greater dread
    Than playing Jeremiah to the worms.
The rights and liberties of yesteryear
    That centuries have barely kept alive
Are preordained to fade and disappear
    By a majority of only five.
Distracted by the carpet's muted threads,
    One hardly hears the falling of the heads.

Sentencing Day

A former federal judge once wrote that "[it] is our duty to see that the force of the state, when it is brought to bear through the sentences of our courts, is exerted with the maximum we can muster of rational thought, humanity, and compassion." However, as even casual observers of the criminal justice system are aware, most sentencers are unaware of or shirk such a duty. According to one prison administrator, at least one-third of the inmates in his institution should not have been sent there. The enormous growth in the penitentiary populations of every state and the federal government is ample testament to the unhappy fact that the judges almost automatically opt for incarceration over any other form of punishment.

Lawyers who represent the least advantaged in our society are painfully conscious that these clients, if convicted, have little chance of avoiding prison, while at the same time middle class or affluent defendants are treated quite differently. For example, a white New York physician who shot a Puerto Rican youth to death in a dispute over a parking space in front of the former's office was given a suspended sentence on the condition that he furnish free medical services to pretrial detainees for a year. At the same time, when an off-duty patrolman, pursuing a black man, was mistakenly killed by a uniformed officer, the fleeing suspect was sentenced to a ten-year term.

In any event, sentencing day is always one fraught with fearful anticipation for both client and lawyer. At no other time is the awful power of the state more pointedly revealed than when it is exercised by a single human being who can destroy the liberty of another person by the utterance of a few words. The years are stripped away in an atmosphere of judicial calm that belies the enormity of the experience for one whose life will most certainly be forever altered.

Like so many other trial attorneys, I have agonized over the vagaries of sentencing, depending so often on what judge the client draws. One lucky defendant may be granted probation or a relatively short prison term while another, with a comparable background and convicted of the identical crime, may receive the maximum the law allows. There is no greater pain than watching unfairly sentenced men and women being escorted out of the courtroom by bailiffs into the unseen world of walls and bars.

That criminal defense attorneys are not alone in such sentiments is evident in recent proposals made by a recent New York State Commission composed of judges, lawyers, a prosecutor, and outside experts. The Commission's members recommended that there be a sentencing chart, or "grid," that would force judges to sentence within narrow limits for given crimes. For example, a first offender convicted of burglary could only be given a term between three and three-quarter, and seven and a half, while one with a criminal record might receive between six and nine and three-quarter years. If a court decided to sentence beyond such limits, it would have to clearly state its reasons for so doing, and off-chart sentences could be appealed by both prosecution and defense. Convicts could earn one-fourth time off for good behavior, but parole would be abolished.

If accepted by the legislature, these proposals would only affect those defendants who elected to stand trial. Of course, they would not be wholly applicable to the 90 percent who opt for plea bargaining. Presumably, the latter would now be forced to dicker for interposing guilty pleas to on-chart crimes, which were lesser than their charges. I do not know whether the proposed "grid" scheme would materially change the present sentencing inequities and I am wholeheartedly opposed to ending parole; but, it at least opens the way for some much needed dialogue in this extremely troublesome area.

Sentencing Day

When court convened at half past nine or so,
    The cast of characters was all in place,
The convict and his counsel in a row,
    The prosecutor's stern official face.
"Impose the maximum," the latter urged,
    And send this man away for twenty years
So that our population will be purged
    Of those who prey upon our inner fears."
Defendant's lawyer then implored the court
    To temper punishment with mercy's guise
And keep his client's prison term as short
    As was consistent with such compromise.
Without a shadow of internal strife,
    The judge deducted half a human life.

Cross-Examination

Some observers have characterized cross-examination as the most reliable method yet devised by civilized society to ascertain the truth in human affairs. Whether it is or not, it can certainly be an ordeal for those subjected to it, particularly when the examiner is an experienced and forceful attorney. Even such an urbane witness as Oscar Wilde, during the trial of his celebrated libel suit against the Marquis of Queensberry, tripped over questions posed to him by one of the latter's lawyers, resulting not only in the loss of his case, but his subsequent conviction for sodomy as well.

Over the years I have learned, often the hard way, that the art of cross-examination can only be acquired by experience. It took a great many trials to teach me that I should never ask key questions unless I knew the answers in advance, and that those beginning with the word "why" must be avoided like the plague. Most importantly, I began to understand that it was vital to avoid taking a hostile crucial witness over his direct testimony again, a course of conduct that generally serves to reinforce his damaging evidence in the eyes of the jury. In other words, only ask questions that do your client some good, and stay away from all others that, at the best, go nowhere and, at the worst, hurt your case.

Cross-Examination

The questions ricochet around the room
    Like rockets detonating in the air,
These harbingers of swift impending doom
    Designed to bring a witness to despair.
Each prior criminal act or carnal sin
    Is thoroughly explored in acid tones
To demonstrate how base the past has been
    And bring to light the closet's secret bones.
Then to the substance of the case at hand
    The lawyer, now a cobra set to slay,
Barks out each harsh stentorian command
    To force a contradiction from his prey.
At last the victim, worn and badly bruised,
    Absorbs the welcome words, "You are excused."

Expert Witness

An expert witness is one who possesses knowledge far beyond the normal life experience of the rest of us. Because of this, such a person is permitted to give his or her professional opinion on the stand, a luxury denied to the ordinary witness. Accordingly, pathologists can theorize about the cause of death, metallurgists the length of time it takes a pistol submerged in water to rust, and forensic odontologists the origin of bite marks on a victim's body. However, it always seems possible to obtain for a price another expert witness who will dispute his colleague's conclusions. The lay jurors must somehow decide which expert is more credible, but for the life of me I have never understood how they do it.

A graphic example of the dilemma faced by jurors in cases where competing and contradictory experts testify took place in the 1983 New York trial of a lifer represented by me who was charged with murdering a female prison guard. Three forensic dentists called by the prosecution swore that a mark on the victim's chest was made by the defendant's teeth, while the same number testifying for the defense either contended that it was not made by human teeth at all or that it didn't match the accused man's bite. Although the jury convicted the man on trial, it is hard to see why the conflicting opinions did not mean that there was a reasonable doubt as to his guilt.

Expert Witness

The witness lumbers to the waiting chair,
    So weighted down with graduate degrees
It takes an hour to lay his background bare
    Before he starts to sell his expertise.
He brings the gifts of science to the aid
    Of those who have agreed to meet his fee,
And promises that, once he has been paid,
    He will achieve forensic victory.
He can identify the victim's blood,
    The killer's teeth, the telltale fingerprint,
The bullet's path, the age of bones and mud,
    And even name the fabric from the lint.
Of course, the other side will find a few
    Who'll swear that quite the opposite is true.

The Litigators

It takes one to know one.

The Litigators

They stride into court like ancient tsars,
    These self-styled paragons of inner worth,
Who see themselves as shining legal stars
    With all the attributes of noble birth.
They vouch no equal in forensic art
    And would put Darrow in the second chair;
They quote themselves to tear the rules apart
    And mangle adverse facts with savage flair.
To them the world is just another stage
    Where they can play a myriad of roles
Which range from simulated sudden rage
    To whispered confidence of kindred souls.
Convinced that they alone can win the day,
    These lions of the law leap to the fray.

Character Witness

The law permits criminal defendants to present the testimony of people who can acknowledge their good reputations for such traits as truthfulness, accuracy, and nonviolence in the community. However, such witnesses are not allowed to give their personal opinions of the defendants. Only highly stylized and artificial accounts of often fictional discussions with others of the defendants' characters are permitted to enhance the subjects' credibility and to portray them as not likely to have committed the crimes in question.

Character Witness

The relative or close confederate
    Intones the oath and, with self-conscious smile,
Sits back, impatient to enumerate
    The golden virtues of the man on trial.
"What is his penchant for veracity,"
    The lawyer asks in soft, expectant voice,
"And is he known in his community
    As one who always makes the legal choice?"
The witness, as rehearsed the night before,
    Pretends to give the question ample scan,
And then responds, with adjectives galore,
    That the defendant is a sainted man.
The jury ponders whether one so free
    Of vice could have committed larceny.

Reading the Will

In some socialist countries there is no absolute right to bequeath property. In the United States, however, as in all other capitalistic societies, not only does such a right exist but it is most zealously guarded. In fact, the laws of most states provide that certain close relatives cannot be disinherited. This sonnet refers to those unfortunate descendants who are not so protected.

Many years ago I found myself surrounded by the heirs of a relatively wealthy single woman who had died rather suddenly while traveling abroad. After making a few small bequests to some servants in her will she had left the remainder of her estate to several animal shelters and a small southern denominational college. I can still recall the steely silence in my office when I had finished reading the dispositive clauses of the will to my anticipative audience. As the testatrix's disappointed relatives filed out of the room, one of them hissed, "I always thought that she was nothing but a selfish bitch!"

Reading the Will

Two weeks have passed since Uncle Henry's bier
    And grief has changed to hopes that soar above,
As those he left behind await to hear
    What value had been placed upon their love.
The lawyer, speaking loud so he'd be heard,
    Intoned the crucial clauses of the will,
As twenty pairs of ears took in each word
    And savored every added codicil.
At reading's end, there was no joy to see
    As Henry's next-of-kin dissolved in shock,
For he had left his all to charity
    Save bric-a-brac and one grandfather clock.
"The no-good bastard," whispered cousin Ben,
    To which his relatives replied, "Amen."

The Chicago Eight

The Trial of the Chicago Eight, as it has come to be known, involved federal charges accusing eight carefully selected political dissidents—David Dellinger, the "aging pacifist"; Abbie Hoffman and Jerry Rubin, "two Yippie chieftains"; John Froines, "a teacher"; Lee Weiner, "a student"; Bobby Seale, "the Panther chair"; and Tom Hayden and Rennie Davis, "the SDS (Students for a Democratic Society)... likely pair"—of conspiring to disrupt the 1968 Democratic National Convention. After Seale was severed from the case in midtrial because of his insistence that he be represented by counsel of choice, the jury acquitted his codefendants of conspiracy, and found only five of them—Davis, Hayden, Rubin, Hoffman and Dellinger—guilty of relatively minor charges.

Judge Julius Jennings Hoffman, a tiny martinet with a voice very reminiscent of that of Jim Backus in the Mr. Magoo film cartoon series, was specially selected to preside at the trial, which began on September 23, 1969 and went on until late February of the following year. From opening day until the day of the verdicts, he did everything in his power, including pointed insults, adverse rulings, and the constant denigration of the defense attorneys, to see to it that the defendants were soundly convicted. In addition, he ordered that Bobby Seale, the only black defendant, be bound and gagged when the latter persisted in vociferously demanding to be permitted to be represented by Charles R. Garry, his long-time attorney, who was recovering from a gall bladder operation.

As soon as the jury had retired to consider its verdicts, Hoffman found all of the defendants and their two attorneys guilty of contempt of court and sentenced them to varying terms of imprisonment. As one of those lawyers, I received the longest sentence—four years and thirteen days—but an appellate court eventually reversed all of the convictions, primarily because of the egregious conduct of the judge and the two federal prosecutors. The highly publicized case did much to mobilize student opposition to U.S. military involvement in Southeast Asia and sparked antiwar demonstrations on many university and college campuses.

It was not until long after the trial that it was revealed, through the Freedom of Information Act, that federal agents had spent hours with the judge before the trial began, predisposing him against the defendants, and inciting him to take strong action against them at the earliest possible moment. When I discovered that this Iago-like tactic had taken place, my attitude toward the judge changed radically, and I ultimately came to regard him as much a victim of governmental misconduct as my clients had been. Although he and I shared the same birthday—July 7—we were more than a generation apart, and I must confess that I felt a certain sadness to learn of his death, just weeks before he would have reached his ninety-first year.

The Chicago Eight

Director Hoover thought the time was due
    To put the New Left on the thorny path,
So he invoked the aid of Nixon's crew
    In directing the Presidential wrath.
From SDS he picked a likely pair,
    And then two Yippie chieftains swelled the list
Filled by a teacher and the Panther chair,
    A student and an aging pacifist.
The trial went on for almost half a year,
    While witness after witness took the stand
To try to justify J. Edgar's fear
    That those accused were perils to the land.
But, at the end, the jury found them free
    Of any traces of conspiracy.

Judge Julius J. Hoffman No. 1

A tiny man who could have won the part,
  In some revised production of Snow White,
Of Grumpy, who is angry from the start
  At everyone who comes within his sight,
His voice as adenoidal as Magoo,
  He read the charges in such scathing tones
That all who heard him somehow deeply knew
  The eight defendants merited the stones.
Throughout the trial, he adhered to his plan
  To miss no chance to let the thought sink in
That, long before the evidence began,
  They all were guilty of a mortal sin.
Just like the Queen in Carroll's *Wonderland*,
  Decapitation was his first command.

Judge Julius J. Hoffman No. 2

At last the old curmudgeon closed his eyes
  And drifted off into the scheme of things,
A victim of what he considered lies
  Set loose by those for whom the truth had wings.
For months he felt that he had held the line
  Against the onslaught of the rebel eight
Who, he had been informed by word or sign,
  Had worked together to destroy the state.
We saw in him the demon's ruddy leer,
  The architect of evil from the bench,
We did not know an artful puppeteer
  Had given every string a hidden wrench.
Perhaps we should have recognized the fact
  That old men seldom see their world intact.

Bobby Seale

Throughout the paneled courtroom's mammoth size,
    The only black defendant's strident voice
Insisted that the system recognize
    His right to have the lawyer of his choice.
The judge was adamant and cried, "Sit down!"
    Whenever he repeated his request,
And let the audience see, by word or frown,
    The court alone, of all the world, knew best.
At last the order from the bench was clear—
    "Take Mr. Seale inside and with him deal
According to the law, then bring him here
    So that this criminal trial does not congeal."
The marshals rushed him back, high in the air,
    His mouth taped shut, his arms chained to his chair.

Jerry Rubin and Abbie Hoffman

These two founders of the Youth International Party (The Yippies) were experts in creating media events that were invaluable in giving the counter-culture of the sixties worldwide publicity. Among other things they dropped dollar bills from the visitors' gallery of the New York Stock Exchange, led many thousands of antiwar demonstrations to the Pentagon for an attempted "levitation" of that mammoth building, orchestrated a "be-in" in New York's Central Park, which was attended by countless waves of young people, and ran a pig for President. Prolific writers and energetic protestors against war, racism, and contemporary mores, they personified the aspirations and accomplishments of the Woodstock generation. I represented them during the Chicago Conspiracy Trial, and at one time or another on a number of lesser charges, as well as before the late unlamented House Un-American Activities Committee (HUAC), where Jerry once appeared dressed in the uniform of a private in George Washington's revolutionary army, and Abbie in a flag shirt.

Today they have gone their separate ways. Jerry has cut his hair and opted for conservative three-piece suits and a business career. The first public sign of his metamorphosis from political activist to mainstream advocate was his employment some years ago by a stock brokerage firm. Now he operates a sort of hiring hall at New York's fabled Studio 54 for young executives on the make. Looking at his cleancut appearance, and listening to his pitch, it is hard to believe that he was once the idol of millions of young people protesting the excesses of the system.

On the other hand, Abbie has remained steadfastly on the firing line. While he was underground because of cocaine charges pending against him, he became one of the leading figures in the fight to prevent industrial pollution of the St. Lawrence River. Since his reemergence, he has interested himself in many of the protests of the day, including those against the CIA's covert war in Nicaragua, and has even visited that beleaguered country. Last June I was arrested with him when we, along with hundreds of others, blockaded the CIA offices in Manhattan, as a demonstration against its Latin American tactics.

In one sense, however, they are still together. Recently they have been touring the country, billed as representatives of the Yippies (Abbie) and Yuppies (Jerry). In their debates, often before large audiences, Jerry emphasizes standard establishment values while Abbie preaches the importance of opposition to what he believes to be the evils of contemporary America. Both men used to proclaim that they could trust no one over thirty; now Abbie, conscious of the high percentage of young people who voted for Ronald Reagan in the past election, has changed that slogan to read, "I don't trust anyone under thirty."

It would be very easy to criticize Jerry for what many regard as nothing short of outright treachery and opportunism, but I cannot bring myself to do so. While I am disappointed by the change in his life style, I am also conscious of the enormous contributions he made to the ending of the Vietnamese conflict. Unfortunately, the system's apologists point to the Jerry Rubins of our time as living proof that the era of the sixties was nothing more than a temporary aberration in our national life and that the return of some of its best-known proponents to the fold amply demonstrates the bedrock value of establishment policies and practices. Because of this unfortunate interpretation, Jerry's defection has been, and will continue to be, a misleading symbol of national retrenchment.

Jerry Rubin and Abbie Hoffman

They showered bills upon the market floor
    To prove that we can't live by bread alone;
They raised the Pentagon a foot or more;
    And named a pig to sit upon the throne.
Their anthem was the beat of rock and roll,
    Their flag the Viet's blue and gold and red,
They dared the snoops of Congress to show soul
    And faced the judges' mandates without dread.
They trusted no one over thirty years
    And dressed like rebels of another day;
They filled their books with hopes and songs and jeers
    And saw to it that humor had its way.
But more than that, they hammered out the rule
    That power must sometimes yield to ridicule.

The Catonsville Nine

The Catonsville Nine was the name given to a number of Roman Catholic peace activists, who were led by Fathers Daniel and Phillip Berrigan. In order to dramatize their opposition to American military involvement in Vietnam, they entered a draft board in a Baltimore suburb in the spring of 1968, and removed and burned some five hundred 1-A files with homemade napalm in an adjacent parking lot. They were later tried and convicted of the destruction of government property valued at more than $100 and sentenced to varying terms of imprisonment. Their prosecution in Baltimore in 1969 was widely reported and served as a catalyst to similar actions by other Catholics in such cities as Milwaukee, Wisconsin and Camden, New Jersey.

During the trial one of the most inspiring episodes I have ever experienced took place. When the defense rested, following the enormously moving testimony of each member of the Nine, explaining why he or she had come to Catonsville, Dan Berrigan asked whether he might lead the courtroom in prayer. The judge, who was caught completely by surprise, did not know how to respond and in desperation turned to Stephen Sachs, the United States Attorney, and asked him whether he had any objection to such a request. "Not only does the government have no objection," replied Sachs, "but we would be glad to join in Father Berrigan's prayer." The defendants, their attorneys, government counsel, the judge, and the audience then rose to their feet and in one voice began to recite the Lord's Prayer. When they had finished, there was absolute silence in the room. It was broken finally by the bailiff's almost whispered command, "Will everyone please sit down," at which we all resumed our seats.

Several years later both Berrigans were accused by FBI Director J. Edgar Hoover of plotting to kidnap and hold Henry Kissinger until the United States withdrew its armed forces from Vietnam. Subsequently, Phillip Berrigan, along with a number of other Catholics, was indicted for this alleged conspiracy, but no one was ever convicted of it. I was one of the lawyers for the Catonsville Nine and my first two grandchildren, one of whom was named after the Berrigan brothers, were blessed by them

while the two priests were serving their sentences in the Federal
Correctional Institution at Danbury, Connecticut.

The Catonsville Nine

With homemade napalm and communal prayer,
    They made their way to where the files were stored,
And marched into the sleeping dragon's lair,
    The loving agents of a loving Lord.
In baskets made for far less lethal trash
    They dumped the symbols of five hundred names,
Then to the parking lot where, in a flash,
    They sought the blessings of the healing flames.
There, arm in arm, they watched the ashes grow,
    While radios began to tell the broadcast band
That they had dared to make some papers glow
    Instead of bodies in an eastern land.
They broke the law, one culprit later said,
    So there would be no increase of the dead.

Wounded Knee

On February 27, 1973, members of the American Indian Movement (AIM), accompanied by local residents of the Pine Ridge, South Dakota, Indian Reservation, left Rapid City, South Dakota, in a caravan of outdated vehicles and headed southward toward the reservation. Although they had initially intended to seize the Bureau of Indian Affairs Building in Pine Ridge, their destination was changed en route to the hamlet of Wounded Knee, where, in 1890, the Seventh Cavalry had massacred some 300 Minnconjou Sioux, and buried their bodies in a common grave that later became a mecca for tourists in that area. After seizing the hamlet, AIM quickly reasserted the reality of the Great Sioux Nation, complete with passports and a governing hierarchy, and dug in for an expected counterattack by the federal government.

As bunkers, road blocks, and other fortifications were hastily erected, a variety of federal forces, including heavily armed FBI agents and United States Marshals, as well as components of the Army and the Air Force, surrounded Wounded Knee. After a seventy-one-day siege, during which one Native American was killed and two federal agents wounded, the occupiers surrendered their weapons and left the area with the assurance that many of the Indians' grievances against the national government would be investigated and, where possible, rectified. It was a promise which, like every Native American treaty, was destined to be broken by the United States shortly after it was made.

During the occupation I visited the Knee—as it came to be known—on two occasions, serving for a brief time as chief negotiator for the Indians. During my second trip in early March, we managed to reach an understanding with the federal forces that resulted in the temporary lifting of the roadblocks. Shortly afterward the AIM leadership conducted an honoring ceremony for a number of people who had played significant roles in the occupation. As soon as the rite was over, everyone marched in single file to the grave of the victims of the 1890 massacre, and as we passed the stone that marked their last resting place, each of us leaned over and touched it. It was undoubtedly my imagination, but when I placed my hand on the monument, I was sure that I felt it move.

The following year I was one of the attorneys for Russell Means, who was tried in a federal court in St. Paul, Minnesota, along with Dennis Banks, for his leadership role in the takeover. During the trial it was revealed that the FBI, among other things, had engaged in illegal wiretaps of the Indians' telephone line, hidden crucial documents and submitted incomplete ones to the court, and suborned the perjury of a number of witnesses. As a result, the trial judge first took custody of the FBI files, and finally dismissed the charges because of massive governmental misconduct which convinced him that "the waters of justice have been polluted."

Wounded Knee

The caravan of trucks and antique cars
    Meandered south throughout the moonless night,
An exodus beneath the passive stars
    That mirrored back the spirit's shining light.
Somewhere along the way the word was passed
    That journey's end would be the common mound
Beneath whose earth three hundred souls were massed,
    The guardians of the liberated ground.
A rawhide drum began its solemn beat,
    In rhythmic cadence to an eagle's scream,
The waiting ghosts were springing to their feet
    As their relations crossed the little stream.
In scores of phantom pipes the birch wood burned,
    In silent joy for those who had returned.

The Oglala Shootout

For at least a decade there has been a virtual reign of terror on South Dakota's Pine Ridge Indian Reservation. Bands of vigilantes, referred to as "goon squads," under the control of a tyrannical tribal chairman as well as Bureau of Indian Affairs (BIA) police officers, according to many observers, have been responsible for hundreds of unsolved murders on the reservation. Since the occupation of Wounded Knee in 1973, the FBI has been widely regarded by Pine Ridge residents as the modern-day equivalent of the United States Cavalry units which, among other things, massacred entire native villages on the Great Plains during the latter half of the nineteenth century.

On June 26, 1975, Ronald A. Williams and Jack R. Coler, two FBI agents who, without advance warning, had approached an American Indian Movement (AIM) enclave on the reservation, and a young Indian, Joseph Stuntz, were killed during a fire fight that eventually involved hundreds of federal agents and BIA officers. Although they were completely surrounded, the handful of besieged Indians managed to escape by following the trail of an eagle, which one of them later claimed had led their way to safety. Subsequently, the four oldest Indian males thought by the Bureau to have been present at the scene—Robert E. Robideau, Darelle Dean Butler, James T. Eagle, and Leonard Peltier—were indicted jointly for the murders of the agents. No one was ever charged with Stuntz's death.

During the summer of 1976, Butler and Robideau, who had pleaded self-defense, were tried together in Cedar Rapids, Iowa, where their case had been transferred because of anti-Indian prejudice in South Dakota. During their trial, in which I represented Butler, a small army of witnesses, including an associate of the United States Civil Rights Commission, testified to the intense fear of unannounced visitors felt by many reservation Indians. Convinced that the defendants had fired at the agents in order to protect themselves, the jury acquitted them both.

Following the verdicts, the government dropped the charges against Eagle "so that the full prosecutive weight of the Federal Government could be directed against Leonard Peltier." After

40

his indictment, the latter had fled to Canada, and was shortly to be extradited by that country on the basis of three affidavits obtained by the FBI from Myrtle Poor Bear, who swore that she had seen him shooting the agents. The government was later forced to admit publicly that all of these documents were false, a concession that led one federal appellate court to characterize their use as "a clear abuse of the investigative process by the FBI."

On April 18, 1977, Peltier was convicted by a jury in Fargo, North Dakota, where his case had been mysteriously shifted, of the murders of the agents, and eventually sentenced to two consecutive terms of life imprisonment. Upon appeal, his convictions were affirmed with the reviewing court finding that although "[T]he evidence against [him] was primarily circumstantial," the "critical evidence" was the testimony of Evan Hodge, a Washington-based FBI firearms identification specialist. Agent Hodge had told the jury that a .223-caliber shell casing found in the open trunk of Coler's car, just a few feet from his body, was extracted from an AR–15 rifle attributed to Peltier. Since the pathologists who had conducted the autopsies on the victims opined that they had each been killed by a high-velocity, small-caliber weapon, such as an AR–15, fired at close and point blank range, Hodge's testimony was extremely damaging to Peltier, and was characterized by the prosecutor in his summation as "the most important piece of evidence in this case."

Long years after the trial Peltier obtained, through the Freedom of Information Act (FOIA), a number of documents relating to the FBI's ballistics examination. On October 2, 1975, a teletype from Hodge to the FBI resident agency at Rapid City, South Dakota, the field office in charge of the overall investigation, stated that a comparison between the .223 casings found at the shootout scene, referred to in FBIese as RESMURS, and Peltier's AR–15, had revealed that the weapon contained "a different firing pin than that in [the] rifle used at [the] RESMURS scene." On the strength of this report an appellate court last April ordered the Fargo judge to conduct a hearing on "the meaning of the October 2, 1975, teletype and its relation to the ballistics evidence introduced at Peltier's trial."

This hearing, at which I, along with John Privitera, Lewis Gurwitz, and Bruce Ellison, represented Peltier, took place in Bismarck, North Dakota, on October 1 to October 3, 1984. Hodge, the only witness produced by the government, testified that by the time of the teletype of October 2, he had only been able to examine seven of the 136 or so .223 RESMURS casings submitted to him for comparison. In fact, he hadn't gotten around to looking at the key casing, which he had received on July 24, 1975, until late December or early January of 1976. However, he freely admitted that he was constantly being importuned by Rapid City to test every .223 casing forwarded to him against any AR–15 associated with the incident of June 26, and that any found near the bodies of the agents should have been examined on a priority basis, given the pathologists' opinion as to the cause of their death. His failure to do so promptly, he explained, was due to a number of factors—the large volume of work associated with the RESMURS investigation, his necessary absences from Washington in connection with other FBI business, and the fact that only he and one assistant were available for firearms identification purposes.

While Hodge was on the stand, we were given an opportunity, for the first time, to look at the handwritten notes of his RESMURS work. In doing so, we noticed that his key report—the one stating that the extractor marks on the .223 casing matched Peltier's AR–15—contained what looked like a far different handwriting than that of either Hodge or his assistant. Accordingly, just before the hearing's end, I asked him whether a third person had worked on the RESMURS ballistics, and he replied that none had. He also insisted that the writing on the report in question was that of his assistant.

We then sought permission to have all of Hodge's notes examined by a handwriting expert. Despite strenuous objections by government counsel, who claimed that this request was "ridiculous," our motion was granted. The original notes were to be examined by an expert selected by us at the FBI Laboratory in Washington, D.C., in the presence of a representative of the government, and the results made part of the hearing record.

An hour after the hearing ended, we were suddenly asked to return to the courtroom. At that time the government, claiming that it had "stubbed its toe," recalled Agent Hodge, who testified that after leaving the stand, he had shown the report in question to his assistant who, unknown to us, had been brought to Bismarck and had been informed by him that the handwriting was not his. Hodge further said that he did not know the identity of the person who had written the document.

The judge, visibly affected by these disclosures, then ordered the government to turn over to defense counsel copies of all of the RESMURS ballistics notes. He also directed that it attempt to determine just who had written the report at issue. Finally, he adjourned the hearing, pending whatever additional evidence developed from the new turn of events. The FBI then forwarded copies of the ballistics notes to us, as well as the name of William Albrecht, Jr., the laboratory trainee who wrote the key report about the matching of the crucial .223 casing and the AR–15. It also disclosed that there were several other such trainees who had assisted Hodge.

On January 7, 1985, Albrecht's deposition was taken in Washington, D.C. He testified that Hodge had been "ecstatic" and "even hugged me" when he said that he had written the key report about the matching of the .223 casing and Peltier's weapon. He also stated that a fourth agent, one Reedman, had also been involved in the RESMURS investigation. It was his opinion that the deaths of two FBI agents would have "a high priority" in the firearms unit, and would be "of personal interest since it is a fellow agent."

In the light of these developments, we asked Judge Benson to open the hearing so that Agents Tardowski and Reedman could be examined by us. He declined to do so, and directed all parties to submit their final briefs. On May 22, 1985, he refused to grant Peltier a new trial [holding that no "constitutional error" had been shown], and the case will soon be returned to the appellate court for review.

On June 25, 1984, three months before the Bismarck hearing, four Soviet Nobel Prize winners, physicists Pavel A. Cherenkov, Nikolai G. Basov, Aleksandr M. Prokhorov, and mathematical economist Leonid V. Kantorovich, signed an appeal to President Reagan on Peltier's behalf. In it they cited his case as "a typical example of politically motivated persecution of Americans who are fighting for human rights. . . ." Putting aside their rhetoric, the laureates, on the face of the record in Peltier's prosecution, shared the appellate court's expressed concern with "the truth and accuracy of Hodge's testimony." If anything, the hearing, with its startling conclusion, raises the specter of a tragic miscarriage of American justice.

43

The Oglala Shootout

When all the weaponry was finally still,
    Two special agents of the FBI
And one young Indian upon the hill
    Had been the victims found to fall and die.
The rest of the beleagured outlaw group
    Escaped the eyes that watched their hopeless flight
By following an eagle's sudden swoop
    Until they reached the safety of the night.
Although the fight began from mutual dread,
    The only ones to face a jury's say
Were those accused of shooting agents dead
    And not the man who blew Joe Stuntz away.
The law, it sadly seems, will always be,
    From time to time, applied selectively.

Auburn Correctional Facility

Built in 1819, the Auburn Correctional Facility, the prototype of American penitentiaries, sits on State Street in downtown Auburn, New York. A sign outside the prison entrance informs visitors that the first electric chair in the country was installed in the institution. Paradoxically, an historical marker, just outside of town, identifies a small house as one formerly occupied by Harriet Tubman, the ex-slave who was one of the organizers of the Underground Railroad, the escape route for runaway slaves prior to the Civil War. Another points out the home of William H. Seward, Lincoln's Secretary of State and an ardent antislavery advocate.

In July of 1929, an Auburn prisoner threw acid in a guard's face, leading to a large scale convict insurrection which resulted in the burning of six prison shops, the destruction of many other buildings, and the killing of the assistant warden. The Attica Correctional Facility, which was opened two years later, was specifically designed to prevent another such uprising. In November of 1970, another generation of Auburn inmates, who had been denied permission to conduct Black Solidarity Day in a prison yard, seized a number of guards, relieved them of their billy clubs and bullhorns, and proceeded to hold a large-scale sitdown. They finally released their hostages and returned to their cells after the prison administration had promised that there would be no reprisals. However, as soon as the rebellion ended, all of its leaders were immediately shipped out to Attica where they were held in solitary confinement.

The failure of the authorities to live up to their promises at Auburn was the main reason for the refusal of the Attica inmates, a year later, to end their occupation of D-Yard until they received the personal assurance of Governor Nelson D. Rockefeller that he would honor any agreement worked out between them and the authorities. Forty-three lives were to be the price of his refusal to make that commitment. Several years later, when I happened to sit next to his daughter Mary at a dinner party, she heatedly asked me why I had once called her father a murderer. When I replied that it was because he had refused to come to Attica, she said he had not done so, he had informed her, for fear that it would have been too dangerous for him to go into the yard. "That was never the issue," I said. "All he had to do was come to the prison, not enter the yard—and he knew that." "I see," she said, and resumed eating her salad.

Auburn Correctional Facility

The prison strides the town's main thoroughfare,
    A brooding paradox of brick and stone,
The first depositary of the chair
    Whose current sears the flesh and chars the bone.
That Auburn was, in its historic past,
    The terminus of Tubman's hidden way,
The place where Seward's higher law was cast,
    Now seems belied by its renown today.
This northern fortress has survived intact,
    The stern antithesis of liberty,
A monument to the unhappy fact
    That some of us are never truly free.
It's sad that we who shape the rocket's thrust
    Have not yet learned to make our system just.

Attica

On September 9, 1971, after months of unsuccessful entreaties to Correctional Commissioner Russell Oswald to remedy conditions at the Attica Correctional Facility, a maximum security New York State penitentiary, 1,289 inmates seized its D-Yard and took some fifty guards and civilian employees hostage. The insurrection began shortly after breakfast and quickly spread when a defective lock on a gate at Times Square, the unofficial name for the junction point of the passageways that led to all four of the institution's cell blocks, gave way under the weight of the prisoners' hands.

The inmates quickly established an Athenian-type democracy with all racial components proportionately represented on its governing council. They then invited a number of outsiders, such as Tom Wicker of the *New York Times*, Clarence Jones of the *Amsterdam News*, Buffalo Assemblyman Arthur O. Eve, and myself, to come to the prison as observers. Most of us responded to their call, and after our arrival the next day, we were permitted to enter D-Yard. We then attempted to mediate the dispute.

For three long days and nights we tried to find a way to bring the confrontation to a peaceful conclusion. After our first visit to the inmates, we hammered out a list of some thirty grievances articulated by them, and finally obtained Oswald's agreement to virtually all of them. However, we could not get approval for the most crucial one—across-the-board amnesty from criminal prosecution—and the prisoners would not settle for less.

It was my opinion that we could not do better than what the officials were willing to grant, and that the rebels' failure to accept the proposed settlement would result in a massive bloodletting. Because the observers felt that Bobby Seale, the Black Panthers' chairman, had enough credibility to obtain the inmates' agreement, we persuaded him to come to the prison. To our great disappointment, he would not make the necessary recommendation without the concurrence of his Central Committee, which could not be immediately convened.

The observers then did everything in their limited power to avoid the impending massacre. For instance, we urged Governor

47

Rockefeller to come to the institution and affirm that the state would live up to the provisions accepted by Oswald, but he refused to do so, a decision that many felt made any nonviolent solution impossible. Led by Tom Wicker and Arthur Eve, we kept haranguing Oswald that force to retake D-Yard would inaugurate a tragedy and that a little more patience might go a long way. Finally, on Sunday, September 12, we entered the yard for the last time, accompanied by a television crew from a local station, and interviewed many of the hostages—all of whom pleaded with the governor that their lives would be jeopardized by an armed assault. Unfortunately, they proved to be accurate prophets.

Early the next morning state troopers, sheriff's deputies, and correction officers, after cannisters of a debilitating gas had been dropped from combat helicopters, stormed into D-Yard and shot to death more than forty prisoners and hostages. I can still recall my horror and shock as I watched these officers, their faces hidden behind grotesque gas masks, and their rifles, shotguns, and machine guns at the ready, rush through the main gate, many of them shouting such epithets as "Save me a nigger!" I could not hold back my tears when I heard the muffled sounds of gunfire coming from the direction of D-Yard and knew that people were dying on its tightly packed earth.

Attica: The Beginning

The day began without the slightest sign
    That it would differ from all those before,
That shortly after the first breakfast line,
    The weight of hands would spring the padlocked door.
Twelve hundred men, a liberating band,
    Looked down upon the ground on which they stood,
And turned a prison yard into a land,
    A most unlikely place for nationhood.
The new electorate, convulsed with dreams,
    Ignored the muzzles of the waiting guns,
And substituted for their inner screams
    The aspirations of their unborn sons.
Emerging from a desperate moment past,
    A man could rise and claim his soul at last.

Attica: The End

The final day began with hints of rain,
    As D-Yard waited for the awesome end
Of what had grown from centuries of pain
    So brother could name every brother friend.
The helicopters soared above the walls,
    Their amplifiers urging all beneath
To heed the message of their strident calls
    And yield the land above the dragon's teeth.
The gas brought tears to unprotected eyes
    As cannisters exploded one by one,
And hostages and inmates sought to rise
    To face the punctuation of the gun.
"Save me a nigger!" was the battle cry
    As troopers marked whose time it was to die.

Martin Luther King, Jr.

I first met this remarkable man in the dining room of the Eldorado Motel in Nashville, Tennessee, on the eve of the 1961 convention of his Southern Christian Leadership Conference. I had been invited to attend the convention by Rev. Wyatt Tee Walker, King's executive director, who, along with hundreds of other arrested Freedom Riders, had been represented by me in Mississippi during the spring and summer of that year. To say that I was surprised at King's appearance would be an understatement. From all that I had read and heard about him, I had expected someone with the guise of an Old Testament prophet. Instead, I found myself across the table from a pleasant-faced, youthful-looking black man, immaculately dressed in a well-tailored business suit. His most distinguishing features were a small, neatly trimmed moustache, high cheekbones, and slightly slanted eyes that gave his face a somewhat oriental cast.

I don't remember what we discussed that night, but during our conversation, I was very much aware that I was in the presence of a most unusual human being. It wasn't so much what he said to me but the manner in which he expressed himself that conveyed this impression. Possessed of a soft, low-pitched voice of unusual resonance, Dr. King managed to give the most routine remark a dignity sometimes far beyond its importance. I don't know whether it was his inflection or his facial expression, or both, but in some indefinable way he made his listener feel that what was being said at the moment was vitally significant.

The next evening I had my first opportunity to hear him address a mass audience. The scene was Nashville's War Memorial Building, a neoclassical structure that sits on one of the city's many hills. I must admit that I was very disappointed by the beginning of Dr. King's speech. I don't know quite what I expected to hear, but I imagine that I had anticipated him to sound like a cross between Jehovah and William Jennings Bryan.

He started out in a low, almost timid voice. As he slowly and methodically transmitted his message calling for a massive voter registration campaign to "change the political structure of the South and the nation," I began to wonder why he had been referred to so often as a great orator. I soon had my answer. Almost before I knew it, I had fallen under the spell of one of the most persuasive voices I had ever heard. Imperceptibly, its cadence quickened and its volume increased as Dr. King, with perfect timing, swept majestically toward his conclusion.

In anyone else his choice of language might have been considered too flowery and his metaphors too far-fetched. But with Dr. King, these became virtues rather than faults. Long before he had finished that night, I was convinced that he was using the finest—and clearest—prose ever uttered.

I wasn't the only one who felt this way. Every eye in the War Memorial Building was glued to this medium-sized, stocky man as he stood on tiptoes, clutching the lectern with both hands for emphasis. His capacity audience was transfixed and, except for an occasional involuntary shout of "Yes, sir!" or "That's right!", there wasn't an audible sound in the huge hall.

When he finished, King stepped back and dropped his hands to his sides. For one breathtaking second, the mammoth auditorium was still. Then pandemonium broke out. As wave upon wave of applause reverberated around the amphitheater, everyone was standing. The conquest was complete.

I have many shining memories of Martin, but there is one that will remain with me as long as I have breath. One night, in Albany, Georgia, he, his wife Coretta, two aides and I were driving back from a church rally to where the Kings were staying when two black men in a Volkswagen flagged us down. "Be careful," one of them yelled, "We heard that there are four white men with rifles looking for Dr. King."

The small frame house was dark when we pulled into the driveway, and because of the warning we had just received, we decided to leave it that way. After pulling down all the shades, we located a candle and set it on top of the upright piano that stood against one wall of the living room.

The minutes began to drag by slowly. Just as I felt that the tension was becoming unbearable, Dr. King stood up and walked over to the piano. "Would anyone care to sing?" he asked quietly. As if we were one person, we rose and formed around the upright. Suddenly, a young woman, who proved to be an excellent pianist, emerged from nowhere. From the moment that she began to play "This Little Light of Mine," the fear and discouragement of the long day disappeared; it was replaced by a transcendental feeling of love and hope for all humanity.

As we sang, I wished that there was some way to remove the roof above us so that the whole world could witness what I was witnessing and feel what I was feeling. I wanted everyone everywhere to listen to five blacks and one white man singing freedom songs by the light of a single candle in a darkened house on a dirt road in southwestern Georgia. An hour after we began singing, we ended with "We Shall Overcome." We linked hands together as we raised our voices. After several verses we hummed the melody while Dr. King asked for our protection from those who would do us harm. When he said, "Amen," we joyously finished the refrain. "Oh, deep in my heart, I do believe, we shall overcome some day."

To say that he had an enormous influence on my life would be the height of understatement: From the day I met him until his murder nearly seven years later, he *was* my life.

Martin Luther King, Jr.

Before we met, I thought that he would be
    A dark-skinned replica of Old John Brown,
A partisan of righteous fantasy,
    A would-be martyr waiting for his crown.
When we were introduced, so long ago,
    I could not bring myself to understand
This smallish man with close-cropped hair would know
    The special route to reach the Promised Land.
That night I heard him preach to all those who came
    To hear the prophet of a new refrain,
And I knew then as well as my own name
    That I would never be myself again.
There is no dream that dies as hard as one
    That seemed so close to being nearly won.

Jack Ruby

After Jack Ruby was convicted in 1964 by a Dallas jury of the murder of Lee Harvey Oswald, the prime suspect in the assassination of John F. Kennedy, and sentenced to death, his brother, Earl, caught up with me at New York's LaGuardia Airport. I was waiting, with Dr. Martin Luther King, Jr., to board a flight to Atlanta. As we were rushing to make our plane, he asked me whether I would join a team of lawyers in an effort to save Ruby's life. When Dr. King, who was then my primary client, stated that he had no objection to my joining the Ruby defense staff, I told Earl that I would do so.

Eventually, I went to Dallas to meet Phil Burleson, Sam Houston Clinton, and Elmer Gertz, the other three lawyers involved, where we worked together on an appellate brief. While we waited for the Texas Court of Criminal Appeals to schedule oral argument, I had a number of talks with Ruby in the Dallas County Jail and learned from him that he had shot Oswald, both to avenge John F. Kennedy's murder and to show that American Jews were as patriotic as anyone else.

The key issue in Jack's appeal was whether a statement attributed to him by a police officer shortly after Oswald's shooting had been properly admitted during his trial. The statement—"I'm glad I shot the son of a bitch!"—was the only evidence of premeditation on his part and had resulted in his being found guilty of capital murder with malice. Without its admission, he could only have been found guilty of a lesser crime which carried a five-year maximum sentence. The Texas Court of Criminal Appeals eventually agreed with us and reversed his conviction. We were preparing for the new trial, which had been transferred to Wichita Falls, when he suddenly died of cancer. A few days later all of the defense team met for the last time in a Chicago cemetery where we served as honorary pallbearers for our tragic client.

Many people, upon learning that I was involved in Ruby's appeal, have asked me whether I believed that he was part of a conspiracy. From my reading of the trial transcripts, I became convinced that he was not. The Dallas police, fearful of trouble, had falsely announced that Oswald was to be moved on that fateful

Sunday from City Hall to the Dallas County Jail at 10:00 A.M., when, in fact, the transfer was scheduled for an hour later. Jack had been awakened that morning by a call from one of the Carrousel Club dancers, who lived in Fort Worth, complaining that she was about to be evicted unless he sent her some money to pay her overdue rent. He had driven to the only Western Union office open on Sunday in Dallas, arriving there shortly before eleven. After sending the money order, Ruby left the office, which was just down the block from City Hall, and was surprised to see a police van backed into its basement ramp. His curiosity aroused, he made his way down the ramp just as Oswald was being escorted toward the vehicle.

The rest is history. Unless he had been told by the police of the actual hour of Oswald's transfer, Ruby could not possibly have known of it. Moreover, if there had been any other customers before him at the Western Union office, or had the clerk been slow in accommodating him, he would have missed Oswald's exit. Lastly, he had taken Sheba, one of his favorite dachshunds, with him and locked her in the car when he went to arrange for the money order. His affection for his dogs was legendary in Dallas, and it is highly unlikely that he would have taken the animal with him if he had intended to kill anyone that day. That he had a gun with him was not unusual, given the fact that, because of the banks' closing after Kennedy's assassination the previous Friday, he had not been able to deposit his club's receipts.

54

Jack Ruby

At dawn the media announced to all,
 Lee Harvey Oswald would be moved at ten
From where he'd spent the night at City Hall
 To a cell in the Dallas County pen.
That hour the night club owner left his space,
 Responding to a dancer's plea for rent,
And drove downtown to find an open place
 From which a money order could be sent.
Emerging on the street, this brooding man
 Looked first toward City Hall, a block away,
And saw, to his surprise, a sheriff's van
 Had backed into the basement alley way.
In ample time to make the evening news,
 He fired once and thus redeemed the Jews.

Joanne Little

A nineteen-year-old black woman, Joanne Little, was arrested in Washington, North Carolina in 1974, and charged with a number of petty thefts of clothing and television sets from a local trailer camp. While she was awaiting trial on these charges, a white jailer attempted to force her to commit an act of sodomy upon him. Rather than submit to his demand, Joanne seized an icepick and fatally stabbed him; then, she fled. After obtaining a lawyer, she turned herself in and was indicted, shortly thereafter, for the jailer's murder. It was a capital crime.

Long before her trial began in Raleigh, North Carolina, where it had been moved, following her motion for a change of venue, her case became a national *cause célèbre*, as church, civil rights, and women's organizations rushed to support her. After a highly publicized prosecution, she was acquitted by an all-white jury. When one of her attorneys was forced to leave the case, I was asked by Jerry Paul, her chief counsel, to replace him, but the trial judge not only refused to allow me to do so but had me arrested for contempt of court when I remarked that "I'm sorry to see that justice in North Carolina hasn't changed much since I was last here." I was referring to a trial in which I had participated a decade earlier in Monroe, North Carolina, during which four activists were convicted of kidnapping an elderly white couple to whom they had given shelter during a racial confrontation in that city.

Years later, I represented Joanne when she was picked up in New York as a fugitive from a sentence she was serving in North Carolina for the thefts which originally led to her arrest. Following a long fight to resist extradition, she was finally forced to return to North Carolina, where she completed her sentence. Today, she is married and living quietly in New York, and, from time to time, drops into my office to say hello. While walking on a Brooklyn street, shortly after she returned to New York, she was mysteriously shot in the chest by an unknown assailant. Fortunately, although the .22 caliber bullet lodged in her heart, she was still able to walk to a nearby hospital where it was removed without any permanent damage. No one has ever been apprehended for this incident.

Joanne Little

A country woman from a backwoods site
    On Carolina's sprawling eastern slope,
She sat by patiently throughout the night
    To face her criminal charges without hope.
They said that she had stolen property
    Worth less than fifteen hundred dollars net,
That she had entered someone's home to free
    Some clothing and a television set.
The jailer waited for the clock to tell
    Him that there was no one awake to see
Before he went into the captive's cell
    To claim from her the last indignity.
No weapon better sapped the tyrant's lust
    Than did her ice pick's liberating thrust.

Karlton Armstrong

For years there had been vociferous opposition by both students and faculty at the University of Wisconsin to the presence on campus of the Army Mathematics Research Center because of their contention that it deeply involved the Madison Institution in the Vietnam conflict. Finally, in 1970, when university officials persisted in their refusal to close the center, Armstrong and three associates exploded a homemade bomb that seriously damaged the building in which it was housed. Although they tried to avoid any bloodshed by calling the police well in advance of the scheduled explosion, the bomb detonated earlier than expected, and a graduate student, working alone in the basement, was killed by a falling beam.

Armstrong, who was later apprehended in Toronto, was extradited to Wisconsin, where he ultimately pleaded guilty to the crime. I was one of the lawyers who represented him at his sentencing hearing, where such antiwar figures as Phillip Berrigan and Daniel Ellsberg testified in his behalf. Although he was given a long term of imprisonment, his institutional record was so good that he was released on parole after serving only a fraction of his sentence. Parenthetically, the sonnet's last line is taken verbatim from Malcolm X's widely publicized remarks about the assassination of John F. Kennedy.

The complicity of many colleges and universities with American foreign policy, particularly during the Vietnam era, was dramatically illustrated when, in the late sixties, students broke into the office of the president of Harvard and pilfered some of his revealing correspondence with the State Department. In addition, the presence of Reserve Officer Training Corps (ROTC) programs on many campuses during that period was a constant source of friction. It is perhaps a sign of the changing times today that ROTC has not only regained its former prestige but is more popular than ever for a variety of reasons, the most significant of which are a rise in jingoism and severe cutbacks in federal funds available for academic scholarships.

Karlton Armstrong

For years there had been protests by the score
    Of university complicity
With those who chose to use an eastern war
    As an advance of foreign policy.
As youthful dreamers trudged from class to class,
    Their counterparts, ten thousand miles away,
Laid down their lives in waist-high grass,
    The lost battalions of a bitter day.
The outrage grew in minds too fresh to know
    That global expectations could excuse
The spreading line of crosses, row on row,
    Competing daily for the nightly news.
Within the spasm of a midnight blast,
    The chickens had come home to roost at last.

Kent State

President Richard M. Nixon ordered American troops in Vietnam to invade neighboring Cambodia in late April of 1970, in order to find and destroy alleged enemy sanctuaries in that country. The invasion, which was characterized by the White House as an "incursion," caused a shock wave of antiwar reaction throughout the country, and as a direct result more than 300 colleges and universities went on strike. The reaction against the Cambodian adventure soon became so intense that the President was forced to terminate it a short time later.

After several days of such protests at Kent State University in northern Ohio, Governor James A. Rhodes sent in a National Guard unit which, on May 4, 1970, in a moment of unjustified panic, fired their rifles from a hilltop assembly area at a group of student demonstrators below, killing four and wounding many others, some extremely seriously. A wire service photograph of a screaming young girl kneeling beside the body of one of the Kent State victims symbolized the national anguish caused by the tragedy. Later on, a teacher and a number of students, including some who had been shot by the guardsmen, were accused of inciting to riot. I assisted in the formation of a legal team, which included former Attorney General Ramsey Clark, to represent them. Eventually, all of the charges were dismissed. Later, a federal civil damage action brought by the parents of the dead students against Governor Rhodes and other Ohio officials was settled for a considerable sum.

In many ways the incident was reminiscent of the so-called Boston Massacre on March 5, 1770, when one member of a squad of British soldiers guarding the Custom House panicked and fired into a crowd of protesting colonists, killing three outright and fatally wounding two others. The crucial difference was that Governor Rhodes, in ordering the Ohio National Guard to the Kent State campus, completely overreacted to student demonstrations against the Cambodian incursion in particular and American military involvement in Vietnam in general—and thereby, set the stage for the ensuing tragedy. The automatic resort by the authorities to force or a show of force at demonstration sites has probably been responsible for more ugly—and sometimes fatal—domestic confrontations over the course of history than any other single cause.

For many years after the tragedy the survivors held an annual memorial ceremony at Kent State. I attended many of these gatherings, but the first stands out most vividly in my memory. Then, Ron Kovacs, a disabled Vietnam veteran, sitting in his wheelchair, which was next to one occupied by a student who had been permanently paralyzed by a guardsman's bullet, leaned over and embraced the latter and shouted, "Now Vietnam and Kent State are united forever!" That moving episode was very much in my mind when I participated some years later, along with a number of Ohio lawyers, in an unsuccessful federal lawsuit attempting to prevent the university from building a gymnasium on the site of the massacre until it could be declared a national monument.

Kent State

The entry in Cambodia caused a shock,
    Reverberating through the campus scene,
As long forgotten keys turned back the clock
    And truth fell victim to a foul machine.
On Blanket Hill, a youthful khaki band
    Watched silently as students made their vow
That to despoil another Third World land
    Could not be tolerated by them now.
The guardsmen froze, their trigger fingers tense,
    As M–1 rifles took a frightful toll
Of those whose only crime was dissidence,
    And four more victims joined the swelling roll.
In one young women's anguished piercing scream,
    The whole world heard the rupture of a dream.

The Execution of Michael X. Malik

When he met Malcolm X in London in 1965, Michael X. Malik, who had been the ruthless agent for a white slumlord in the British capital, immediately and drastically changed his way of life. In time he became the executive director of Black House, a center designed to assist ghetto dwellers in their struggle for survival and a decent life. Several years later he returned to his native Trinidad and established an agricultural commune some thirty miles north of the capital city of Port of Spain, which was visited and supported by many political activists, including John Lennon and Yoko Ono.

On February 20, 1972, while Malik and his family were visiting his wife's relatives in Guyana, a mysterious fire seriously damaged their home, and firemen claimed that they had found the bodies of two murdered people buried in the vicinity. Malik was one of four suspects charged with the crimes, and in a trial in which a juror favorable to him was poisoned, he was convicted of one of the murders and sentenced to death. After the failure of his appeals, he was hanged, despite pleas to Queen Elizabeth II by many well-known people, such as Massachusetts Senator Edward M. Kennedy, for a commutation of his sentence. In order to prevent demonstrations at his execution, the Trinidadian authorities hanged him on a Friday rather than the traditional Tuesday.

At the request of the Lennons, Attorney Margaret L. Ratner and I visited Malik in his Death Row cell and engaged appellate counsel for him. On a subsequent trip we were not permitted to see him again. To this day many informed observers believe that the case against him was fabricated by Trinidad's prime minister, the late Eric Williams, who feared him as a potent political rival.

The Execution of Michael X. Malik

In Trinidad they hang at Tuesday dawn,
  Except for those whose ends they cannot wait,
And these are spun into the darkness on
  Whatever is the most convenient date.
The Royal Jail sits in downtown Port of Spain,
  A monument to Britain's heavy hand,
The gallows squat astride a heat-drenched plain
  That serves for soccer when no deaths are planned.
On May sixteenth, the Caribbean sun
  Commenced its ordained journey to the west,
Content to ride the rote meridian
  And let the sleepy hangman do the rest.
A murderer or martyr, time may tell
  If he has earned his heaven or his hell.

Ralph D. Abernathy

Ralph Abernathy was apparently destined to walk always in Martin Luther King's footsteps, even though he was an older and a more experienced pastor. In Montgomery, Alabama, the organizers of the boycott of that city's buses, following the arrest of Rosa Parks for refusing to give up her seat twice for a white patron, selected King over Abernathy and a number of other black clergymen as the protest's titular leader. As a result of the successful conclusion of the boycott, King became nationally known and later events made his name a familiar one throughout the world.

Abernathy was his second-in-command until King's assassination in 1968, when he succeeded him as president of the Southern Christian Leadership Conference. Despite the fact that he was always in King's shadow, he emerged, after the latter's death, as an enterprising and couragous leader in his own right, escorting a mule through hostile police lines during the demonstrations surrounding the 1968 Democratic National Convention in Chicago, and visiting the besieged Native American occupiers of Wounded Knee five years later. However, as time has already proved, history is certain to regard him simply as a stand-in for his more celebrated comrade.

I remember him best when he agreed to appear as a witness for the defense during the Chicago Conspiracy Trial. When Judge Hoffman refused to allow him to take the stand because, due to airport traffic congestion, he had arrived in the courtroom a few minutes late, his response was as pertinent as it was eloquent. As he put it:

I left Chicago yesterday after being informed that the court had ruled that I could not testify in this case. I left heavy of heart because I had interrupted my overloaded schedule and traveled through sleet and snow to tell what I knew to this jury, only to be refused the right to do so because I was sixteen minutes late in getting to the courthouse. I cannot close this statement without saying that I have returned from abroad as an ambassador of good will for my country's system of justice and equality, where I groped for words to explain that both existed. When foreigners said, "You have no democracy, no justice in America," I attempted to prove that we did. After my experience yesterday in this court, I can no longer defend my country against such attacks.

Ralph D. Abernathy

A stolid, thoughtful, soft-tongued preacher-man,
    He always looked a little out of place,
As if some old and unseen master plan
    Had relegated him to lesser grace.
Sometimes, he seemed to rise beyond his role
    And catch the fire that lit the leader's trail,
Until the stresses of his ponderous soul
    Made the wished-for illusion swiftly pale.
Then in the flash of the assassin's gun,
    He found the pulpit left to him by right,
Yet even then he could not be the sun
    But just a lost and lonely satellite.
Caught in the shadow of a brighter flame,
    He found his glory in reflected fame.

H. Rap Brown

H. Rap Brown, or Jamil Abdullah Al-Amin as he is known today, had been a friend and client of mine ever since he first became chairperson of the Student Nonviolent Coordinating Committee (SNCC) in 1967. I have represented him in all of his many criminal prosecutions, and out of the contact engendered by this relationship, an extremely close personal association has developed. He was married in my home, and we have spent many hours together discussing the problems of the world and, in particular, the oppression of black people in this country. After he had succeeded Stokely Carmichael as SNCC's fourth chairperson, he quickly inspired headlines when, following his shooting by a deputy sheriff during a demonstration in Cambridge, Maryland, he stated that "violence was as American as cherry pie."

As a result of his abrasive militancy, he was soon charged with a battery of state and federal charges designed to neutralize him as a force in the black community. In addition, he was grievously wounded by a New York police officer, who fired at him while he was lying helpless on the ground. A graphic example of the virulence of the hatred directed against him can be seen in the remark made by a federal judge who was scheduled to try a case against him. At a meeting of the Louisiana Bar Association, shortly before the trial began, the judge said that he hoped to keep his health because he "wanted to get that nigger." Fortunately for Brown, his subsequent conviction before the judge in question was reversed because of this remark.

H. Rap Brown

As tall and thin as Irving's Ichabod,
    He burst like Mercury upon the scene;
An heir to those who bore the master's rod,
    He knew the slavery of the years between.
On every front the system sought his end
    By hook or crook or gun or court decree,
Embarking on a plan to make him bend
    And march in cadence with the semifree.
But finally one night they brought him down,
    A policeman's bullet in his underside,
The latest casualty to sink and drown
    Beneath the water of a hateful tide.
He sparked the vengeful lightning by his cry
    That violence here was just like cherry pie.

People v. William R. Phillips

In 1970, John V. Lindsay, then the mayor of New York, alarmed by reports of widespread police corruption, established a body, known as the Knapp Commission, to investigate it. Detective William R. Phillips, who admitted extorting protection money from prostitutes and others, had obtained evidence for the commission, which implicated other officers; he was a star witness at televised hearings in late 1971. While Phillips was testifying, another detective saw him on camera and came to the conclusion that he resembled a composite drawing done by a police artist of a suspect in the murders of a pimp and a prostitute on Christmas Eve, 1968. As a result Phillips was charged with the killings, thus aborting much of the Knapp Commission's work.

Phillips's first trial, at which he was represented by F. Lee Bailey, resulted in a hung jury of ten to two for acquittal. At his second trial, he was convicted and eventually sentenced to twenty-five years to life. After the verdicts it was inadvertently discovered by the defense that one juror, John Dana Smith, had applied for and vigorously pursued an investigator's job with the District Attorney's Office shortly after his selection. The trial judge, however, although condemning the prosecution for keeping silent about the matter, denied Phillips's motion for a new trial.

Although I have never met Phillips, I did file a federal habeas corpus petition on his behalf, claiming that he could not have received a fair trial with John Dana Smith on the panel that convicted him. The judge to whom the petition was assigned granted it, and ordered Phillips's release unless he was retried within ninety days. After this ruling was affirmed by an intermediate Federal Appellate bench, in a six to three decision the Supreme Court reversed, holding that Phillips had had a fair trial. Not only does this ruling amply illustrate the ideological leanings of the Court's majority, but it flies in the face of all law and logic. As the dissent put it, "A juror who was almost certainly prejudiced against [Phillips] participated in the deliberations. If due process really does mean a full and fair opportunity to be tried by an unbiased jury . . . then in this case, due process has been denied." These words were cold comfort to a man who must now spend the best years of his life in prison.

People v. *William R. Phillips*

The juror was selected for the trial
    When all the counsel thought that he'd be fair,
Not knowing he would soon decide to file
    For a position in the D.A.'s lair.
Before the end, the prosecutor learned
    The juror's application was in house,
But quickly ordered everyone concerned
    To keep as silent as the fabled mouse,
Then, when the case was done and fully tried,
    And truth, by chance, first saw the light of day,
The judge refused a plea to set aside
    The vote and rule defendant's guilt away.
The high tribunal voted, six to three,
    To sanctify this immorality.

People v. Lemuel Smith

Donna Payant, a white guard at one of New York's maximum security prisons, was strangled to death on May 15, 1981, and her body was smuggled out of the institution in a garbage truck. Some time later Lemuel Smith, a black prisoner serving two life sentences for murder, was accused of the crime. After a lengthy trial in Poughkeepsie, New York, during which C. Vernon Mason, Mark Gombiner, and I represented him, Lemuel Smith was convicted and sentenced to die under the state's only remaining death penalty statute. On July 2, 1984, New York's highest court held the statute to be unconstitutional since it did not provide for the consideration of mitigating factors insofar as punishment was concerned, a ruling that was recently affirmed by the United State Supreme Court. I wrote this sonnet during a hiatus in the trial, after I had learned that the state's only electric chair was located in the same prison where Donna Payant's death had occurred.

People v. Lemuel Smith

The trial drones on from day to endless day,
    Each one a repetition of the last,
As witness after witness has a say
    To recreate facsimiles of the past.
The lawyers spin their wealth of words
    To extract answers or restate the law;
Spectators come and go like hungry herds
    In search of tasty fodder for their maw.
The judge keeps order from his perch on high,
    Recording each decision on his list,
The jurors rise and leave and then draw nigh
    To wonder what their absent ears have missed.
Just miles away, the long neglected chair
    Sits patiently within its voltaged lair.

Death Penalty Oral Argument

The New York Court of Appeals, the state's highest tribunal, re-
served its entire session for oral argument in the case of Lemuel
Smith on April 23, 1984. At issue was the constitutionality of the
country's last remaining mandatory death penalty statute—that
affecting life termers who kill. I wrote this sonnet on the train
back from Albany to New York City, hours after both sides had
completed their respective presentations before the seven-mem-
ber bench.

What was on my mind was the theme expressed in the conclu-
sion to the lengthy brief submitted to the court on Lemuel Smith's
behalf—that the taking of a life by the state violated the funda-
mental ethos of any purportedly civilized society. The lawyers—
Mark and Robert Gombiner, Ronald L. Kuby, C. Vernon Mason,
Peter J. Avenia, and I—had expressed ourselves as follows:

In creating this brief, counsel for the defendant could never forget, for a
solitary moment, that a human life was riding on their words. Morever,
its drafting was punctuated by the highly publicized executions of a num-
ber of condemned men in other states as well as several dramatic elev-
enth-hour reprieves in parallel prosecutions. At the same time we were
aware of the growing reluctance of a majority of the United States Su-
preme Court to permit full appellate review in capital cases and the in-
credible comment of Chief Justice Warren E. Burger, in denying a stay,
that defense lawyers in such cases were "seeking to turn the administra-
tion of justice into the sporting contest that Roscoe Pound denounced
three-quarters of a century ago."

We were also quite conscious that millions of our fellow citizens, ter-
rified by what they perceived to be an inexorable rise in the number of
violent crimes in their local communities, were blindly turning to the res-
toration or extension of capital punishment as a panacea for their fears.
Despite the undeniable fact that there is no conclusive evidence that the
death penalty plays any role whatsoever in deterring criminal homicides,
it appeals to the irrational frenzy periodically generated in our collective
psyche when the bitterness and frustration born of seemingly endless
terror in the streets combine to overwhelm and subvert the thinking pro-
cess. Even as we penned these pages, we well knew that, throughout the

nation, there was a rising and insistent chorus of frightened voices clamoring for the ultimate in retribution in every case in which a life was unjustifiably taken.

Lastly, we were painfully cognizant that our client was widely regarded as a pariah, hated and feared by even those who opposed capital punishment in the general sense, although the trial evidence conclusively proved that he did not murder Ms. Payant. As the *New York Times* stated in an agonized editorial, captioned, "The Death Penalty's Hardest Case," following the imposition of sentence: "Of the 1,200 prisoners under sentence of death, New York has only one. But that condemned man, Lemuel Smith, has caused more destruction than most, and he promised nothing but anguish to those who would spare him from the electric chair. His brutal crimes make him Exhibit A for capital punishment and a great burden for its opponents." We realized that, in the hearts and minds of virtually everyone who may read or hear our arguments in his behalf, the life of this one black man had little if any redeeming social value and what Supreme Court Justice William J. Brennan, Jr. recently characterized as the "fatal conclusion" of his appeal would leave hardly any mourners in its wake.

Yet despite the subtle but very real influence of this known hostile environment, we completed our task in the earnest hope that this tribunal, New York's highest judicial voice, would seize the nettle and prevent, for the moment at least, this state from joining the list of those which have opted for death over life and murder over mind. If our labors help to save the life of Lemuel Smith, then they will have been well worth every second, minute, and hour of the planning, research, and writing that went into the creation of this plea for sanity and justice. If they serve to raise appreciably the level of the ongoing public debate on the morality of the taking of a life by the sovereign, then they may have contributed much to the possibility of the eventual triumph of reason over rage, a result that will have infinitely more significance than whether Lemuel Smith follows Donna Payant into death.

On July 2, 1984, the Court of Appeals ruled that Lemuel Smith's death sentence was unconstitutional, and, eight months later, the Supreme Court denied the prosecution's petition for review, following which the defendant was re-sentenced to another term of life imprisonment.

Death Penalty Oral Argument

The judges asked their questions with a zeal
    Reserved for arguments of great import,
As if they knew exactly how to deal
    With controversies of a major sort.
At issue was the power of the state
    To still the beating of a human heart
Whose owner had incurred the bitter hate
    That is reserved for those a breed apart.
The court indulged itself in logic's quest
    To find a rule of law to solve the game,
Unable to confront the waiting test
    Of whether ethics had a greater claim.
This is the way we shall at last go down—
    Two-legged lemmings with no choice but drown.

Malcolm X

I first met Malcolm X (El-Hājj Malik El-Shabazz) in the early sixties when I served as the moderator of a radio debate between him and a New York psychiatrist. I was so impressed by his performance that I made it a point to stay in close contact with him, and we were friends until he was shot to death by assassins in Harlem's Audubon Ballroom on February 21, 1965. A week before his murder his home in East Elmhurst, Queens, New York, had been partially destroyed by a bomb blast. Both incidents occurred just after Malcolm had returned from a trip to Mecca with a new and conciliatory attitude toward whites, and he and Dr. King had agreed to work together in their common struggle against racial oppression.

Shortly after Muhammad Abdul Aziz (Norman 3X Butler), Khalil Islam (Thomas 15X Johnson), and Mujabid Abdul Halim (Thomas Hagan or Talmadge Hayer) were indicted for Malcolm's murder, Halim's family asked me to represent him. Because of my relationship with Malcolm, I could not do so. Ironically, many years later, Halim invited me to visit him in prison, and when I did, he told me that Aziz and Islam were innocent of the crime. The killing, which was the result of the hatred of many of the followers of Elijah Muhammad toward Malcolm because of the latter's personal attacks on the Nation of Islam leader, was planned and executed by Halim and four other New Jersey Muslims, who were motivated by their deep devotion to the man who had founded their sect.

After Halim had furnished me with all the details of the assassination, including the names and descriptions of his four accomplices, I tried, without success, to set aside the convictions of Aziz and Islam. During the course of my investigation, I interviewed many people, including Benjamin Karim (Goodman), the man who preceded Malcolm at the lectern on the day of his death. As a result I became convinced Halim was telling the truth and that two unfortunate men have been kept in prison for more than twenty years for a crime they could not possibly have committed. If any inmates ever merited commutations of their sentences, these two do.

At this juncture it is difficult to describe my feelings about Malcolm. Before I met him, I was appalled by the cutting edge of his rhetoric, and I probably shared the feelings of most whites that he was a truly dangerous demagogue. As time went by and our acquaintance deepened, my feelings of uneasiness dissipated, and I began to understand that he was accurately expressing the bitterness and frustration justifiably felt by a substantial segment of the population. He dared to say out loud what many others thought but kept to themselves, and if his condemnation sounded harsh or grating to white ears, it was no less legitimate and no more strident than that of Frederick Douglass a century earlier.

Nevertheless, underneath the public man was a warm and responsive human being. Once I asked him to grant an interview to a white reporter from a suburban weekly who was a victim of cerebral palsy. He not only agreed to do so, but sat for hours while the writer stammered out his questions. The patience and understanding behind Malcolm's willingness to give up so much time for a physically handicapped small-town journalist belied his platform appearance and more than proved his inner worth to me.

Malcolm X

To some he was a black and shining prince,
     Articulating centuries of rage,
With curses for the past and awful hints
     Of retribution from the Prophet's page.
But others saw him in a different light,
     A demagogue aglow with racist fire,
Consumed with hatred for the color white
     And eager to ignite the vengeful pyre.
A black Messiah or a man of wrath,
     The difference has little meaning now;
He trod the bitter stones of slavery's path
     In hopes the pain would fade away somehow.
Just as he glimpsed a newer, better day,
     A spate of bullets tore his life away.

Adam Clayton Powell, Jr.

Adam Clayton Powell, Jr., who represented Harlem in the House of Representatives for many terms, finally became, by virtue of seniority, the chairman of its powerful Education and Labor Committee, then a single unit. As such, he wielded more political clout than any black person, then or now, has ever achieved. I first met him in 1967, after his colleagues had voted to exclude him from the Ninetieth Congress for allegedly deceiving the House about travel expenses and making illegal payments to his wife. After his exclusion, he called me to his office, gave me a check for $2,500 and asked me to form a legal team to fight to regain his seat. He then flew off to his favorite Bahamian retreat of Bimini, where he spent most of his time sipping scotch and milk and playing dominoes at a local bar. Within a week Arthur Kinoy, Jean Camper Cahn, Herbert O. Reid, the late Frank Reeves, and I had joined forces to represent him, both before the Congress and in the courts. Eventually, the Supreme Court found that "the House was without power to exclude him from its membership," but the struggle had taken its toll, and a short time later he died of a broken heart, literally and figuratively.

I was one of the few people invited by Powell to attend his son's wedding to a socially prominent white woman in Washington. He appeared at the cathedral, resplendent in his clerical robes and wearing the medallion given to him by Ethiopia's Haile Selassie. He was apparently not asked to participate in the marriage ceremony, and I could sense the deep disappointment felt by him as the rite wore on. A few years later, when I viewed him lying in his coffin at the Abyssinian Baptist Church, where he had reigned for so long, all I could think of was the pain he must have experienced that day in Washington.

Adam Clayton Powell, Jr.

A tall and handsome man with skin so fair
    He could have easily passed for white;
Instead he chose to voice his Savior's prayer
    Where hopes soared higher than the slumlord's blight.
The faithful guaranteed his sure return
    To Washington on each Election Day
Until his senior status let him earn
    The transient power of the gavel's sway.
No black had ever reached such heights before
    And quickly, in the Harlems of the land,
The feeling grew that he could fulfil more
    Than those who called the piper's tune had planned.
At last his colleagues, sensing danger near,
    Destroyed him with the piety of fear.

Leroy "Nicky" Barnes

Barnes, who was once depicted as the reigning monarch of the Harlem drug trade, was convicted of a number of serious violations of federal narcotics laws in 1977 and sentenced to life without parole. After all of his appeals had failed, he contacted the government, and offered to testify against many of his claimed former associates. As a result of his cooperation, a grand jury indicted eight men, seven of whom went to trial in the fall of 1983. I represented one of these defendants, and while Barnes was on the stand testifying for the government, I wrote this sonnet.

The use of informers serving long prison sentences to support criminal charges against other defendants had become so prevalent that I wanted to emphasize my own feeling that no one should be convicted upon the word of witnesses who have nothing to lose and everything to gain by perjuring themselves. Frank Lopez, the attorney for a codefendant at the trial, read the poem as I was writing it and requested permission to use it in his summation. He recited it to the jury from memory, and although our clients were convicted, the jury was out for more than four days. I hope that the sonnet at least had some effect, no matter how transient, when the panel was considering the credibility of "Nicky" Barnes.

Leroy "Nicky" Barnes

He takes the oath with all the pious hope
    Of genuflecting priests before the cross,
This fallen emperor of drugs and dope,
    In one last hustle to reduce his loss.
Condemned to spend his life without parole,
    Interred in maximum security,
He saw his chance to scramble up the pole
    And salvage what was left of breathing free.
His captors said, if he would take the stand
    And testify against alleged allies,
That they would see to it that his demand
    For leniency was viewed by proper eyes.
How judge the credibility of one
    With naught to lose and so much to be won!

Readbacks

Every trial lawyer knows the agony of sitting through extensive readbacks of testimony when requested by a deliberating jury. Not only is the process an extremely tedious one, with the court reporter intoning, normally in a seemingly endless monotone, words that were spoken weeks—and sometimes months—ago, but it subjects the attorneys to frustrating repetitions of questions that should never have been asked or were either ineptly put or not adequately followed up. The particular readback referred to in the poem occurred in a New York case in which two former Black Panthers, Abdul Majid and Basheer Hameed, were accused of murdering a police officer who was shot to death in his squad car in April of 1981. The jury eventually split eight to four for acquittals, the second panel to fail to reach verdicts.

Readbacks

The jury's two-line note was terse yet clear:
    "We'd like to have the testimony read
Of witnesses who said that they were near
    The moment when the victim was shot dead."
The teenaged girl who watched, in shocked surprise,
    Secure behind her second-story blind,
The cabbie who could not believe his eyes
    As terror froze the corners of his mind.
The jurors waited in their tiny crypt,
    Impatient to be further edified,
While lawyers worked to isolate the script
    Of those who, weeks ago, had testified.
The court reporter, in staccato voice,
    Raced through the pages of the panel's choice.

J. Edgar Hoover

Following extensive hearings, the Senate's Church Committee revealed, in 1974, that the FBI's first director had resorted to at least several decades of indecent covert action programs, under the acronym COINTELPRO, against many dissident groups and individuals. The latter included virtually the entire black protest movement as well as those elements of the white community which supported it. Using scurrilous or provocative anonymous letters and telephones calls, disruptive *agents provocateurs*, and surreptitious listening devices, to name only a few of the many dirty tactics employed, the FBI strove to discredit such persons as Dr. King (whom Hoover publicly denounced as "the biggest liar in America"), Malcolm X, Elijah Muhammad, H. Rap Brown, and Stokely Carmichael, as well as their organizations, supporters, and sympathizers. One particularly vile operation involved the sending of an anonymous communication to a *Los Angeles Times* gossip columnist, alleging that white actress Jean Seberg, who had attended a Black Panther Party fundraiser, was pregnant by a member of that militant group. When the columnist published the false information, Jean Seberg lost her baby and, as a direct result, eventually committed suicide.

In an exhaustive analysis of COINTELPRO the Church Committee found that between 1956 and 1971 the FBI had conducted

"a sophisticated vigilante operation aimed squarely at preventing the exercise of First Amendment rights of speech and association. . . . [M]ost of the techniques used would be intolerable in a democratic society even if all of the targets had been involved in violent activity. . . . The American people need to be assured that never again will an agency of the government be permitted to conduct a secret war against those citizens it considers threats to the established order."

Unfortunately for Jean Seberg and so many others, the awakening came much too late.

J. Edgar Hoover

He raped the Constitution every day,
  This megalomaniac who learned his trade
By withering the Bill of Rights away
  As he pursued each brutal Palmer raid.
His enemy was anyone who dared
  To criticize his sainted FBI,
He could not stand the sight of those who shared
  A common goal to right the bigot's lie.
There was no dirty trick he would not use
  To halt, defame, deter, or terrorize
Those citizens who did not share his views
  Or saw their country's goals through different eyes.
There is no villain like a fool possessed
  With certainty that he alone knows best.

Puerto Rico

Since I have represented many people who believe wholeheartedly in independence for Puerto Rico, such as Carlos Feliciano and Vicente Alba, I have made it a point to learn what I could about that troubled island and its history. Given its status by the United Nations several years ago, it is now an American colony in a world where colonialism is fast becoming an anachronism. It currently exists as a convenient source of cheap labor, a tax shelter for stateside corporations, a firing range and refueling station for our Navy, and a playground for those wealthy enough to afford its Condado vacations.

Discovered for Spain by Columbus in 1493, Puerto Rico was first colonized by Ponce de León, who was appointed its governor seventeen years later. Sugar cane was introduced in 1515, and within three years the first black slaves were imported to cut and process it. Initially, however, the Spanish were far more interested in gold than sugar but had exhausted every bit of the metal the island had to offer in 1570, and sugar production became its main industry. In 1898, following the end of the Spanish-American War, it was ceded to the United States, and nearly twenty years later, the passage of the Jones Act extended American citizenship to all Puerto Ricans, whether they wanted it or not.

Both under Spanish and American dominion, Puerto Ricans have exercised steady pressure for independence. Spearheaded by the late Don Albizu Campos, the *independentista* movement has persisted for almost a century, gaining significant momentum since the end of World War II, despite every effort by the United States to inhibit or destroy its leadership and, at the same time, convince the rank and file that their future lies with either statehood or a continuation of the commonwealth status. Yet, the drive for self-determination is stronger than those who exploit the island would have the rest of us believe, and it may well be only a matter of time before there is a new nation in the Caribbean.

Puerto Rico

To Spain it was a port to guide the helm
    Of ships sailed forth to plunder half the earth,
An outpost of a predatory realm,
    Greed-bent to loot the New World's hidden worth.
With shot and sword and icons on a pole,
    The mother country forged its slavers' bands,
And sent its galleons to collect the dole
    Created by the work of shackled hands.
Four centuries along the future's course,
    The new *conquistadores* replaced the old;
With tax exemption as their driving force,
    They mined a greater and a brighter gold.
As tourists walked the ways of ancient kings,
    An island nation waited in the wings.

The Judge's Charge

At the very end of every jury trial, the bailiffs lock the courtroom doors while the judge lectures the panel on the applicable law. As one who has sat through hundreds of these sessions, I still don't see how jurors manage to understand the legalese to which they are subjected. In a few states, like Maryland, they are not bound to apply the law to the facts before them, but in most they must follow it. I am convinced that, more often than not, the court's instructions, in whole or in part, are incomprehensible to them.

There is a doctrine, often referred to as jury nullification, which, simply stated, means that the jurors sometimes deliberately disregard the law because of the compelling nature of the case. For example, in the famous 1735 New York trial of John Peter Zenger, the colonial printer accused of defaming the province's British governor, the jury acquitted the defendant despite the fact that the evidence against him, under the then existing law, was conclusive. In the trial of the Catonsville Nine, I was prevented by the judge from using the exact words of Andrew Hamilton, Zenger's attorney, who in his summation exhorted the jury to use their consciences in deciding his client's fate. Nevertheless, I firmly believe that jury nullification provides a viable alternative to applying what the community may regard as an oppressive, unjust, or unworkable law.

The Judge's Charge

At last it was the judge's time to act
    And educate the jury on the law
It was to square against each proven fact
    To reach a verdict or declare a draw.
Before His Honor cleared his throat to bore
    The panel seated in a double row,
The bailiff closed and locked the courtroom door
    So that no sound would mar the legal flow.
His voice droned on for hours without end,
    Defining every what and where and why
In terms as difficult to comprehend
    As those they were supposed to clarify.
The jurors, nearly nodding in their pew,
    Gave silent thanks when their ordeal was through.

Freedom Riders

The Congress of Racial Equality (CORE) organized in the spring of 1961 what soon came to be known throughout the country as "Freedom Rides." Blacks and whites would board interstate buses in the North and ride them together below the Mason-Dixon line. As soon as they arrived in such places as Birmingham, Alabama, and Jackson, Mississippi, they would be quickly arrested and charged with disorderly conduct or breaches of the peace. In Birmingham, Public Safety Director Eugene "Bull" Connor led that city's crackdown on these Freedom Riders or "mixers," as he called them; in Jackson, Captain J. L. Ray served that function.

When the number of those arrested in the latter city had reached over a hundred, I was asked by the American Civil Liberties Union (ACLU) to assist Jack Young, the harassed black Mississippi lawyer who was representing all of the defendants. While I didn't know it then, my trip to Jackson represented the start of my connection with the effort to end racial oppression in the South. With Carl Rachlin, the CORE general counsel, and Young, I tried *State of Mississippi* v. *Henry Thomas*, the test case that eventually resulted in the end of the use of local criminal statutes to enforce segregation on interstate carriers.

The incident that abruptly pushed me into the struggle was when I witnessed the arrest of five Riders at the Greyhound bus station in Jackson the day after my arrival. When Young told me that a new shipment of Riders was expected that morning, I walked to the station, which was filled with police officers and reporters, and sat down at the lunch counter. A few minutes later all of us at the counter were ordered to move by an officer. As I complied, I saw three young white women, a white man, and a black youth enter the terminal from the direction of the loading ramp.

The quintet, after hesitating for a moment at the sight of the roomful of policemen and media representatives, walked over to the side of the lunch counter that I had just vacated. A man who I later discovered was Captain Ray met them as they sat down on the now empty stools. "I'll ask you just once," he said firmly, "to leave the station. If you do not, you will be arrested." There wasn't a word from the Riders, and Ray waved at his waiting men. "Okay," he barked, "take 'em away!" In a matter of seconds the five were escorted out of the depot and into a waiting paddy wagon.

As I walked back to Young's office, my head was whirling. For the first time in my life, I had been privileged to watch an action of total commitment, and I sensed that I would never be quite the same again. The sight of five frightened young people who had traveled long and far in order to offer their bodies, quietly but forcefully, as a witness to the equality of all people had taught me what I had never known before—that only by personal involvement on behalf of others is it possible to justify one's own existence.

Freedom Riders

It all seemed very simple, without fuss,
> To buy a ticket with a nonwhite friend
And sit together on a southbound bus
> Until they reached their far-off journey's end.
In Birmingham "Bull" Connor vowed to halt
> The integration of the open road
And apprehended those whose only fault
> Was to insist upon an equal code.
At Jackson, Mississippi, Captain Ray,
> Surrounded by his waiting police,
Charged interracial riders every day
> With scores of varied breaches of the peace.
But neither fear nor clubs nor county jails
> Could stay these travelers from their freedom trails.

V.C.O.s

In virtually every metropolitan courthouse aging retirees, with plenty of time on their hands, can be daily found watching trials, giving unsolicited advice to attorneys and parties alike, or exchanging notes in the corridor during recesses. Generally referred to by court personnel as V.C.O.s, for Veteran Courthouse Observers, they find their free escape from boredom in the varied human dramas being enacted before them. Every trial lawyer soon gets to know who they are, and many rely on their opinions of how the case is progressing and what result can be expected from a particular judge or jury. They also are a prime source of often fascinating courthouse gossip, and sometimes they accidentally overhear conversations that are extremely helpful to one side or the other.

V.C.O.s

They go from room to room on each court day,
    These ancient relics of another age,
To find their entertainment in the fate
    Of some poor actor on their daily stage.
They know each lawyer's voice and dress and style
    And which one judge will titillate them more,
They search for life down every courtroom aisle
    And look for zest in any corridor.
They are the critics of each drama played
    To final scene before their waiting eyes;
They understand the shock of errors made,
    The triumph of the shrewdly planned surprise.
They find the plight of someone else's son
    The stimulus to lives so nearly done.

St. Augustine, Florida

During the celebration of its quadricentennial in the early spring
of 1964, St. Augustine, Florida, supposedly the oldest American
city and one of its most rigidly segregated, became the scene of a
number of sit-ins at its white-only motels. The protests, organized
by the Boston affiliate of Dr. King's Southern Christian Leader-
ship Conference, eventually led to the arrest of Mary Elizabeth
Peabody, the wife of a ranking Episcopalian bishop and the
mother of the then Massachusetts governor. Along with the late
Tobias Simon, a Miami attorney, I represented Mary Elizabeth
Peabody and her fellow demonstrators, and we eventually suc-
ceeded in having the charges against them dismissed. There was
great publicity generated by their arrests, as well as from the daily
confrontations between blacks and whites on the city's segre-
gated beaches and at the ambuscade of Dr. King's quarters by
night riders which followed them. Finally, on July 4, President
Lyndon B. Johnson signed into law the Civil Rights Act of 1964,
a far-reaching statute that prohibited discrimination in most areas
of public accommodations.

I first met Mary Elizabeth Peabody and her scores of fellow
demonstrators at the St. John's County Jail. I had gone with Si-
mon to select and interview witnesses for a scheduled hearing
before a federal judge to whose court we had removed their cases
on the theory that they were being prosecuted for doing acts per-
mitted by the Constitution. Peabody, an angular woman with
wispy white hair, seemed none the worse for her two days in jail.
She quickly grasped the rationale of our legal position and eagerly
awaited our questions. "I hope that I'll do all right," she said when
we finished. "I've never done this before."

At the hearing the next morning she testified that she had not
come to St. Augustine with the intention of being arrested. In
fact, on her first day in town she had left the dining room of the
Ponce de León Motor Lodge, where she was eating with a black
friend, when asked to do so by the manager. But first she had
made the sheriff read the Florida undesirable guest statute to her.
"It's a very long law with a great many words in it," she recalled,

"and I realized that I couldn't fit some of those parts . . . that described why I should leave."

The next day she had decided not to depart, a decision that led to her arrest. "We began to feel that we were pretty cowardly to leave our friends taking the brunt of this," she told the judge. "At first we thought that we could make our witness without breaking this particular ordinance which we do not have in Massachusetts, and which we therefore do not think is in accordance with the Constitution, but finally we decided we would rather stand up for the Constitution than we would for the ordinances of the city of St. Augustine."

After her release she spoke at a mass meeting at St. Augustine's First Baptist Church. There were many speakers that night, but I remember Mary Elizabeth Peabody most vividly. I don't know whether she had ever attended such a gathering before, but it was obvious that she was deeply moved by the experience. "I am so glad I came down to St. Augustine," she told the packed church. "I couldn't stay safe in Boston while you were suffering here. But I know in my heart that I didn't do anything for you— you did everything for me. You helped to give my life purpose and meaning, and when I go back tomorrow, I want to leave behind my most heartfelt gratitude. Thank you all so very much."

St. Augustine, Florida

The nation's oldest town, its boosters swear,
    In competition for the tourist trade,
Replete with patios and palm-lined square
    And waters to restore one's youthful shade.
Today there is no outward sign of strain
    Between the ancient city's black and whites
To conjure up the days of rage and pain
    When bloody clashes were among its sights.
In '64, a Boston bishop's kin,
    Accompanied by a non-Caucasian friend,
Refused to leave a segregated inn
    And brought an evil era to an end.
Sometimes it takes the courage of a few
    To teach the rest of us just what to do.

Contempt of Court

I have been held in contempt by so many courts that it is difficult to remember all of the occasions. In some instances I have spent an hour or so in custody; in others, I have spent as much as a weekend in the cooler. Fortunately, the longest such sentence imposed on me—the four years and thirteen days decreed by Judge Hoffman in the Chicago Conspiracy Trial—was reversed on appeal, thanks to the efforts of my perennial attorney in these matters, Morton Stavis.

Despite the widespread notion that I deliberately court contempt citations, the fact of the matter is that I do not. However, there are some actions by judges which, in my opinion, are so wrong and so hurtful to my clients' interests that I feel compelled to speak out and, indeed, believe it is my duty to do so. Judicial tyranny is no more to be tolerated than that of any other public official, and I will continue to risk imprisonment whenever judges cross the bounds of what I consider to be acceptable conduct.

My philosophy in this regard was perhaps best expressed by me in my remarks to Judge Hoffman just before he sentenced me in Chicago in 1970:

Your Honor, I have been a lawyer since December of 1948, when I was first admitted to the bar in the state of New York. Since that time I have practiced before, among others, the Supreme Court of the United States, the United States Court of Appeals for the First, Second, Third, Fourth, Fifth, Sixth, Seventh, Tenth, and District of Columbia Circuits, Federal District Courts throughout a great deal of the United States, and the United States Court of Military Appeals, as well as a host of state tribunals.

Until today I have never once been disciplined by any judge, federal or state, although a large part of my practice, at least for the last decade, has taken place in hostile southern courts where I was representing black and white clients in highly controversial civil rights cases.

Yesterday, for the first time in my career, I completely lost my composure in a courtroom, as I watched the older daughter of David Dellinger being rushed out of the room because she clapped her hands to acknowledge what amounted to her father's farewell statement to her.

I felt then such a deep sense of utter futility that I could not help crying, something I had not done publicly since childhood.

I am sorry if I disturbed the decorum of the courtroom, but I am not ashamed of my conduct in this court, for which I am about to be punished.

I have tried with all my heart faithfully to represent my clients in the face of what I consider—and still consider—repressive and unjust conduct toward them. If I have to pay with liberty for such representation, then that is the price of my beliefs and my sensibilities.

I can only hope that my fate does not deter other lawyers throughout the country, who, in the difficult days that lie ahead, will be asked to defend clients against a steadily increasing governmental encroachment upon their most fundamental liberties. If they are so deterred, then my punishment will have effects of such terrifying consequences that I dread to contemplate the future domestic and foreign course of this country. However, I have the utmost faith that my beloved comrades at the bar, young and old alike, will not allow themselves to be frightened out of defending the poor, the persecuted, the radicals and the militants, the black people, the pacifists, and the political pariahs of this, our common land.

But to those lawyers who may, in learning what has happened to me, waver, I can only say this: stand firm, remain true to those ideals of the law which, even if openly violated here and in other places, are true and glorious goals, and, above all, never desert those principles of equality, justice, and freedom without which life has little if any meaning.

I may not be the greatest lawyer in the world, your Honor, but I think that I am at this moment, along with my colleague, Leonard Weinglass, the most privileged. We are being punished for what we believe in.

Contempt of Court

The lawyer raised his voice in great surprise
    At the outrageous ruling from the court.
"What you have done will sanctify the lies
    Of perjured witnesses," was his retort.
His Honor winced at counsel's angry tide,
    His cheeks turned red with fire from within,
He waited for the torrent to subside
    Before he punished for a cardinal sin.
"I find that you have gone beyond the pale,"
    He roared in tones so scathing that they steamed,
"And sentence you to do two weeks in jail
    To learn that judges must not be demeaned."
As bailiffs rushed the culprit to be caged,
    Judicial dignity had been assuaged.

Fannie Lou Hamer

Fannie Lou Hamer, a black sharecropper from the Mississippi Delta, and her husband were evicted in 1962 from their Ruleville farm by their landlord because they attempted to register to vote. From that day to the end of her life, she was a political activist, seeking to obtain the franchise for blacks, first in her home at Sunflower County and then throughout the state. One of the founders of the Mississippi Freedom Democratic Party (MFDP), an interracial coalition created to challenge the white only regular Democrats, she and her colleagues forced the 1964 National Democratic Convention to acknowledge, to some degree at least, their demand for delegate recognition. In 1965, I was one of the lawyers who, under the direction of Morton Stavis, represented the party's almost successful effort to unseat the state's all-white congressional delegation, a project in which Fannie Lou Hamer was intensely involved. Blessed with a beautiful contralto voice, she sang such freedom favorites as "This Little Light of Mine" and "Go Tell It on the Mountain" at rallies and demonstrations throughout the country in support of this and other related projects.

In April of 1963, Hamer and five other Black women tried to obtain service at the lunch counter of the bus station in Winona, Mississippi. The group, which was returning home from a voter registration workshop in Charleston, South Carolina, was arrested and held in jail for four days. During their imprisonment they were beaten by policemen with night sticks and whipped with leather straps by two black trusties who had been ordered to do so by the officers.

The next year she was nominated by MFDP for her district's congressional seat. When the State Board of Elections refused to place her name, as well as those of all other MFDP candidates, on the official November ballot, they ran in a Freedom Election at which anyone possessing the qualification required by Mississippi law was permitted to vote without discrimination as to race. They all received an overwhelming majority of the votes cast. Sometimes symbolic victories can be as heartening as real ones.

When I had gotten to know her better, I once asked her why she risked her life, her health, and her well-being so often, and she replied that she was paying back a debt to Mickey Schwerner, Andy Goodman, and Jim Chaney, the three civil rights workers who had been murdered in Mississippi in June of 1964. "If those three boys could die for me," she said, "then I must do what I can for my brothers and sisters." Until she worked herself to death at age fifty-eight a few years later, she more than did what she could.

Fannie Lou Hamer

It's hard to think that she is really dead,
    This doughty lady with the booming tones,
Who tried, with song, to reach the fountainhead
    And wake the conscience of the torrid zones.
She earned the hatred of those who swore
    Few blacks would ever register to vote,
So that the South could stay forevermore
    The white plantation owner's table d'hôte.
Reared in the Mississippi Delta's loam,
    She spread the gospel of equality
In town and country worlds away from home
    Wherever there were ears to hear her plea.
Until she closed her eyes, her little light
    Exposed the darkest corners of the night.

The National Lawyers Guild

Formed originally in 1937 as an alternative to the highly conservative American Bar Association, which did not then admit black attorneys and took the most reactionary positions on the political and legal issues of the time, the NLG is today an association of some 7,000 lawyers, law students, and legal workers. It is dedicated to the safeguarding of civil rights and liberties, both in the United States and throughout the world. Because of the successes of its members in defending political dissidents, as well as the organization's consistent and vociferous libertarian stands, the government sought, during the Cold War of the fifties, to place it on the Attorney General's infamous "List of Subversive Organizations," an attempt that, largely because of the Guild's strenuous opposition, ultimately failed to attain its objective. Throughout its existence it has been in the forefront of the struggle to make America live up to the guarantees of its Constitution, and I am proud to be one of its members—even if it subjects my office to sporadic break-ins, wiretaps, and physical surveillance by the FBI.

The National Lawyers Guild

In sharp reaction to the ABA,
    This brotherhood and sisterhood began,
Designed to give the law an even play
    And resurrect the Constitution's plan.
Because of its success, it fell from grace
    Almost as soon as it announced its start,
And was earmarked for an intended place
    Upon the government's subversive chart.
This band of legal workers tries to make
    The goal of equal justice for us all
Much more than just a slogan to forsake
    To meet the needs of those who run the hall.
The Guild is just one small but strident voice
    Of those who give the brave a decent choice.

The Constitution

This sonnet contains references to four stages of the black experience after the American Revolution. The first, in which each slave was counted in the new Constitution as three-quarters of a person in calculating the number of Representatives allotted to the southern states, was brought to an end by the bloody Civil War. A generation later, after the all too brief but highly inspirational Reconstruction Era, the doctrine of "separate but equal" was created by the Supreme Court to legitimize a return to official racial discrimination. In 1954, the same tribunal reversed itself in the famous case of *Brown* v. *Board of Education of Topeka, Kansas,* and declared that the segregation of public school children on the basis of race was unconstitutional. In recent years, however, the Court has begun to cut back sharply in such areas as affirmative action programs and the access of civil rights litigants to the courts, while at the same time making it more difficult to prove purposeful discrimination, and extending the doctrines of sovereign, judicial, and prosecutorial immunity from suit.

The Constitution

No glowing word or phrase could ever hide
    That blacks were fractions of humanity,
A faceless, nameless, unseen, unheard tide
    To those who swore they loved equality.
A million died to end hypocrisy
    And bring the bondsman's era to an end;
But then the courts concocted a decree
    That separation was the proper trend.
It took another sixty years before
    The ancient paragraphs received full sway;
Today the promised freedom may once more
    Be suddenly interpreted away.
This document, so filled with noble prose,
    Must seem to some a trifle comatose.

The Great Emancipator

When I was growing up, it was often impressed upon me, both at home and at school, that Abraham Lincoln was a saint among men. After all, he had freed the slaves and preserved the Union; and, before and during his Presidency, he had given a great number of remarkable addresses. On the other hand, his murderer, John Wilkes Booth, was universally regarded as a consummate villain whose criminal act had immeasureably delayed the postbellum reconciliation of North and South.

As I grew older, I began to understand through my own reading and analysis that the Lincolnphiles had successfully marketed a wholly misleading portrait of the sixteenth President of the United States. The Emancipation Proclamation, far from being a true humanitarian instrument, was nothing more than a pragmatic war measure, designed to raise flagging northern morale in the wake of an almost unbroken string of Confederate military victories. Moreover, it purported to free "all persons held as slaves within any State . . . the people whereof shall then be in rebellion against the United States," while ignoring those held in areas under Union control. The hypocrisy of the document can best be seen in the President's angry revocation of the order of General David Hunter of May 9, 1862, in which the latter had declared that all slaves present on the Union-held islands off the coast of South Carolina were "free forever."

On August 14, 1862, barely a month before the drafting of the Proclamation, Lincoln summoned a number of black leaders to the White House. In an incredible display of overt racism, he told them that "you and we are different. We have between us a broader difference than exists between almost any other two races. . . . This physical difference is a great disadvantage to us both. . . . But for your race among us, there could not be war . . . on this broad continent, not a single man of your race is made the equal of a single man of ours." He informed his listeners that he had appropriated funds to buy land in the Chiriqui coal region of what is now Colombia and urged them to lead their people there. When the President's remarks, faithfully recorded by Benn Pitman in his new shorthand, were published by the press, Frederick Douglass assailed his "pride of race and blood, his contempt for Negroes, and his canting hypocrisy."

Four months later Lincoln signed a contract with white promoters to resettle 5,000 black volunteers on Haiti's Isle of Vache. By May of 1863, only 450 recruits had been found, and they were exported to their new home. The experiment was an abysmal disaster, due to corrupt white management, an outbreak of smallpox, starvation, mutiny, and the hostility of the Haitian government, and the President was finally forced to send a ship to return the survivors to the United States.

Shortly before the end of the war, Lincoln had created a reconciliation plan to be put into effect as soon as hostilities ceased. One aspect provided that if 10 percent of those who voted in 1860, in any seceded state, would "make a sworn recantation of [their] former unsoundness," and pledge allegiance to the United States, they would be permitted to establish a civilian government, elect representatives to the Congress, and have their state restored to the Union with full federal protection. In other words, since those who voted in 1860 were limited to white males, the President was offering to return the old order to power in exchange for a simple oath. Had this plan been put into effect, the great Reconstruction Era would possibly not have occurred and the ex-slaves would have been little better off than they had been before the war. In one sense, the bullet from Wilkes's derringer, although he hardly intended it to do so, might well have salvaged the struggle's moral gains.

The Great Emancipator

The Great Emancipator did not free
    The slaves he had the power to liberate,
But chose instead to grant their liberty
    To those enthralled in each seceded state.
He wanted to get rid of every black
    By sending them 2,000 miles away,
So distantly that they could not come back
    And thus remove the causes of the fray.
Then, when the war was coming to an end,
    He mouthed a reconciliation plan
That if a fraction of the whites would bend
    Their knees, they would control their realms again.
Historians delight to make it clear
    That martyrs' sins must quickly disappear.

Rosa Parks

In early December, 1955, Rosa Parks, a black seamstress in Montgomery, Alabama, boarded one of the city's buses. Rosa Parks, who had been Christmas shopping, sat down in the nonwhite section, which was designated as such by a movable marker attached to the rear of one of the seats. When the white section was filled, the driver moved the dividing marker back several rows and ordered Parks, whose seat was now in the white section, to move further back, which she did. A few minutes later, as additional homeward-bound white shoppers boarded the bus, the marker was moved once more, again making it necessary for Parks to give up her seat. When she refused to do so, the driver stopped the bus and had her arrested.

The news of her arrest galvanized the black community into action. The Montgomery Improvement Association (MIA) was quickly formed with Dr. Martin Luther King, Jr., the new pastor of the Dexter Avenue Baptist Church, selected as its president. Under his leadership a boycott of the city's bus system began, which lasted for 382 days until segregation on the line was brought to an end. The success of this nonviolent tactic made Dr. King a national figure and inaugurated his career as a civil rights leader.

I had the honor of awarding the first Rosa Parks award, established by King's Southern Christian Leadership Conference, to Dr. William G. Anderson, the osteopath who had led the 1961–62 Albany, Georgia, demonstration against racial oppression in that city.

The Legend of Rosa Parks

Montgomery's Christmas season was in swing
    With buyers filling every downtown shop.
Toward night the carolers began to sing
    As crowds surged to the place the buses stop.
On one, the whites soon overflowed their space
    While there was room in that reserved for black;
The driver, conscious of his debt to race,
    Twice moved the color marker to the back.
The tired seamstress could not fail to hear
    A second call to give her seat away,
But overcame four centuries of fear
    And told the driver she was there to stay.
Unheard by her, a thousand choirs sang—
    From such a simple act, a movement sprang.

Setting the Fee

Anyone who has been hit with a substantial legal fee will certainly identify with this sonnet. Legal fees have gotten so exorbitant that even so conservative an observer as Supreme Court Justice Sandra Day O'Connor recently told a law school audience that "the gap between the need for legal assistance and the ability to pay for it seems to be widening. Costs of legal services have escalated beyond the means of many people. My impression is that the gap should be narrowed by lawyers volunteering to help where help is needed without regard to the possible compensation."

What Justice O'Connor overlooks is the fact that the fees paid for legal services to indigent defendants have been pegged so low that most private lawyers cannot afford to represent such clients. Until very recently, in New York, for example, the authorized rate in felony cases was $25 an hour in court and $15 out, with an extremely low maximum except when the court has determined the matter to be one of an exceptionally difficult or complicated nature. On the federal side such fees, partially because of a 1983 strike by District of Columbia trial attorneys, have just been raised to $60 and $30 respectively, a welcome and much needed change.

Setting the Fee

No sooner had the client described his case
    With full and adequate sufficiency,
Then did the lawyer don an earnest face
    And sigh, "Now to the matter of my fee."
"I've never sought such legal help before,"
    The subdued client solemnly replied.
"I need to have some help upon that score
    And hope that you will be my learned guide."
The lawyer coughed and started to explain
    How much it cost to meet his overhead
And why this case would need his might and main
    If justice were to be adroitly led.
He paused, a thoughtful look upon his brow,
    Then charged the most the traffic would allow.

The Arrest

This sonnet was the result of my shock at learning of the arrest of my client, Fulani Sunni-Ali (Cynthia Boston), an initial suspect in the attempted holdup of a Brinks armored car in Rockland County, New York, on October 20, 1981. Several days later Sunni-Ali was apprehended, along with her five young children, in a rural Mississippi farmhouse by an army of some 200 FBI agents, supported by armored vehicles and helicopters. Quickly spirited to New York by her captors, she was soon freed when it was discovered that it was physically impossible for her to have been in New York on the day of the crime.

The Arrest

At first there are the knocks upon the door
    That sound like claps of thunder in the night,
And then the silence of the tomb before
    You rise and manage to turn on the light.
The raps resume and grow much louder still
    Until it seems that they will wake the dead;
Your heartbeats sound like a pneumatic drill,
    Your lips go dry with paralyzing dread.
The door unlocked, two men burst into sight
    With cries to freeze the least of their commands;
One rattles off each set Miranda right
    While his companion quickly cuffs your hands.
Then comes the shattering reality
    That all at once you are no longer free.

Court Reporters

There can be no doubt that, armed with the transcript of a trial, lawyers are far better able to prepare their summations, to say nothing of improving cross-examination. However, the charges for what is referred to as "daily copy"—a transcript of that day's testimony—are astronomical, and few clients can readily afford them. Yet, it is beyond question that for a truly fair trial, particularly on the criminal law side, daily copy is indispensible. In this area indigent defendants are often better off than middle class ones since many courts, albeit reluctantly, are inclined to grant the former's application for such transcripts when the prosecutor has ordered them.

The Court Reporters

At the appointed hour every day,
    These scribes emerge from cubicles unseen,
And to their courtrooms make their steady way,
    Equipped with pen or stenotype machine.
With hieroglyphics meaningless to all
    But those acquainted with their arcane lore,
They sit by silently until the call
    To read a word or phrase that went before.
They do not, for a moment, stay their hand
    And interrupt summations at their best,
To change a roll, locate a rubber band,
    Or just to let their weary fingers rest.
And if you need their marks deciphered clear,
    They charge you more than Shakespeare earned a year.

Corporate Law Firms

There are a number of extremely large law firms, boasting hundreds of partners and associates, which represent most of the country's major corporations. With their superbly appointed quarters, armies of stenographers, typists, investigators, paralegals, messengers, and file clerks as well as batteries of the latest in business machines, out-of-town and foreign offices, engraved stationery, and hierarchical structures, they are prototypes of what most lay people believe to be the norm. Generally quite conservative in everything from politics to dress, they recruit their annual crop of neophytes from the top ranks of the country's most prestigious law schools.

While many of these giants permit some of their junior partners or associates to do what is sometimes referred to as *pro bono* (for the public good) work, it is usually limited to "safe" cases. It is very rare indeed to find such lawyers involved in any highly controversial litigation, and I can't remember meeting any large firm personnel in the criminal prosecutions growing out of the Freedom Riders' arrests, the occupation of Wounded Knee, the Attica prison rebellion, or the activities of the Black Panthers or Puerto Rican nationalists, to name but a handful. This is unfortunate as it prevents bright, talented, and socially conscious young attorneys from furnishing vital services to prospective clients sorely in need of them.

Corporate Law Firms

Their senior partnerships exceed a score,
    Their hordes of juniors wait to climb the stair,
Their steno pools are larger than a corps,
    Their stationery is engraved with care.
They shepherd mergers through the SEC,
    Assisted by a wealth of legal tact,
And try to safeguard each monopoly
    From application of the Sherman Act,
They search for loopholes in the taxing norms,
    And recommend just when to sell or buy;
They march to court in pinstriped uniforms
    To fight until the client's well runs dry.
These high-priced minions of the corporate state
    Compute their soul into their billing rate.

SNCC

In 1960, Ella Baker, then Dr. King's executive director, helped to organize the Student Nonviolent Coordinating Committee (SNCC) as the youth arm of his Southern Christian Leadership Conference (SCLC). Its founding statement proclaimed its commitment to "the philosophical or religious ideal of nonviolence as the foundation of our purpose, the presupposition of our belief, and the manner of our action." Referred to everywhere by its acronym, pronounced "Snick," it soon became an autonomous group which served as the cutting edge for many of SCLC's operations throughout the South. Its first four chairpersons—John Lewis, James Forman, Stokely Carmichael, and H. Rap Brown—became nationally known for their militancy and courage.

Over the years I worked very closely with Howard Moore, Snick's general counsel, and at one time or another appeared in courts in Georgia, Alabama, Mississippi, North Carolina, Louisiana, Virginia, Maryland, and Tennessee for its members. On St. Patrick's Day, 1965, I represented it at a celebrated late-night conference in the County Courthouse at Montgomery, Alabama, attended by Forman, Martin Luther King, and a number of local officials in a successful effort to avoid further violence in that city. Twenty-four hours earlier a raid by mounted sheriff's deputies on black and white college students demonstrating in front of the state capitol had taken place and eight of them had been hospitalized. At other times, I was an admiring spectator at many of Snick's organizing activities in Albany, Georgia, and Selma, Alabama—to name but a few areas of its involvement.

SNCC

A band of dreamers longing to breathe free,
    They fanned throughout the country's southern tier,
Determined to confront reality
    With all the promises of yesteryear,
Despite the lies of those who called them reds,
    They tried to break the last of slavery's code;
They persevered through bloody, broken heads
    To march along a dark, forbidden road.
They were the front line troops who bore the blows
    Of those who vowed the South would never yield,
And placed their bodies where their ardent foes
    Were forced to kill them or give up the field.
They sang that there was freedom in the air,
    And did their best to spread it everywhere.

Grand Jury

The Grand Jury is an institution that began in England in the twelfth century. Once referred to as the Grand Inquest of the Nation, it was originally designed to be a buffer between persons suspected of crimes and the state. In essence, no one could be forced to stand trial for life or liberty unless a majority of fellow citizens had found probable cause of guilt.

On these shores the Constitution states that "no person shall be held to answer for capital, or otherwise infamous crime (felony), unless on a presentment or indictment of a Grand Jury. . . ." However, in recent years, grand juries, both state and federal, have become, in large measure, rubber stamps for prosecutors who completely dominate their proceedings. Among other things, the latter control the areas to be investigated, the choice of witnesses, and the direction of their testimony, and the selection of the crimes for which indictments are sought. Although the Grand Jury is supposedly an independent investigative body, it is rarely, if ever, properly informed of its powers in that respect, and the result is a slavish dependence upon the prosecutor for guidance.

On the federal level, the agency has now become a convenient device to harass political dissidents by incarcerating them, usually without a jury trial, for their failure to cooperate with it. For example, knowing that many supporters of Puerto Rican independence, as a political act of faith, will not testify before grand juries, the government has subpoenaed them, and upon their anticipated refusal to testify, succeeded in jailing them for contempt. Subpoenaed witnesses are even denied the right to raise their constitutional privilege against self-incrimination as the government may now confer upon them a limited immunity to defeat such a contention. In addition, the secrecy in which the proceedings are conducted prevents lawyers from accompanying their clients into the hearing room.

Small wonder that the Tudors' infamous Court of Star Chamber, where many of the same tactics were employed, comes quickly to mind.

Grand Jury

Conceived to be a shield between the state
  And those suspected of a legal breach,
It has become a potent tool of late
  To punish those who opposition teach.
No lawyers are permitted on the spot
  Where those subpoenaed walk their lonely mile,
And who must answer every question shot
  Or be condemned without a jury trial.
The patriots who sanctified the right
  To remain silent on the witness chair
Would rotate wildly through their endless night
  To learn their words had vanished in the air.
Like England's chamber with its roof of stars,
  None but the victims see and feel the scars.

The Harlem Six

The Harlem Six were a group of black youths who flew pigeons together from a Manhattan rooftop. In April of 1964, they were arrested and charged with the murder of the white proprietor of a Harlem clothing store and the serious wounding of her husband. The chief witness against them was a Robert Barnes, who claimed that, while he had participated in the plan to rob the store, he had dropped out before the crimes took place.

The mothers of the defendants joined together to support their sons, and author Truman Nelson wrote a book, *The Torture of Mothers*, about their efforts, while James Baldwin and other Harlem luminaries soon came to their aid. Although the youths were saddled with appointed lawyers they did not want, and were found guilty at their first trial, an appellate court eventually reversed their convictions in 1968. Their second trial resulted in a hung jury, as did their third, with the panel in the latter voting seven to five for acquittal.

After the last trial, where I represented one of the remaining four defendants (a fifth had pleaded guilty to manslaughter and was soon released, while another, Robert Rice, was tried alone and convicted), Barnes wrote to me and asked me to visit him in prison where he was serving a sentence for an unrelated crime. When I did so, he executed an affidavit in which he said that he had been forced by the police to testify falsely against the defendants. As a result of his recantation, the prosecutor, in 1972, permitted the four, now young men, to plead guilty to a lesser crime and be immediately released. Unfortunately, Rice was not included in this settlement and is now in his twenty-first year of imprisonment.

The Harlem Six

The clothing store was still that April day
    When youthful blacks came through the silent door
And asked to see some trousers on display
    Before they killed the white proprietor.
The police at once arrested six young men
    Who flew their pigeons from a Harlem roof,
And said that they had broken up a den
    Of murderers without a shred of proof.
It took three trials and seven years of time
    Before the witness who had turned them in
Confessed that he had never seen the crime
    And then had lied in court to save his skin.
There is a tragic postscript to this tale—
    Though five are out, a sixth remains in jail.

Lenny Bruce

During the latter part of his life, Lenny Bruce, who had been one of the country's most biting and satiric comedians, became utterly obsessed with litigation. This change in his once ebullient personality was undoubtedly due to the many obscenity charges brought against him in such cities as Los Angeles, Chicago, and New York, most of them based on his suggestive use of a broom handle during his act. Shortly before he died, in August of 1966, he came to me and asked me to institute federal lawsuits against the many prosecutors whom he thought were persecuting him. Before I could even decide whether he had viable causes of action, he took an overdose of drugs in California and was found dead in his bathroom, his arms wrapped around the toilet bowl.

Lenny Bruce

The prosecutors never understood
    That what they thought to be profane and lewd
Were just reflections of the bad and good
    With which our social system is imbued.
He made a broomstick seem a work of art
    To those who saw the humor of it all,
But to the policeman's bland official heart
    It was the symbol of the Devil's call.
He used the prophets, gods, and seers of old
    To liberate the laughter of his quest,
But ran afoul of those who saw no gold
    In stripping halos from their saintly rest.
He mortgaged his iconoclastic soul
    And died, his arms around a toilet bowl.

Assata Shakur

Assata Shakur, once known as Joanne Chesimard, a poet and for-
mer member of the New York Black Panther Party, was indicted
for seven major crimes, including murder and bank robbery, in
the late sixties and early seventies. In six of these cases she was
either acquitted or the charges were dismissed. However, in the
seventh, the alleged murder of a New Jersey State trooper, she
was convicted of being present at the scene of the incident when
a companion, under unknown circumstances, shot and killed the
victim. At the same time another occupant of the vehicle in which
she was riding at the time of the trooper's death, Zayd Shakur,
was also shot to death.

Along with a number of other attorneys, I represented her at
her trial in New Brunswick, New Jersey. Although she was finally
convicted and sentenced to life imprisonment, there was ample
evidence that she had not been involved in the shooting and had
herself been seriously wounded during the gunplay. There is a
strong probability that the jury found her guilty because of the
unceasing prejudicial publicity identifying her as the "Queen of
the Black Liberation Army," (BLA), which the authorities con-
stantly fed to a compliant press.

In November of 1979, Assata Shakur escaped from prison and
has never been recaptured.

Perhaps the best gauge of Assata's sensibilities is her poetry,
which appeared in book form in 1980. One poem, in particular, to
her daughter Rema, who was born in jail on July 14, 1976, Bas-
tille Day, should prove my point. It reads:

There was no star
No Manger
No wise men bearing gifts
To welcome your brown life
Into this world

There were no trust funds
No Nannys
No elegant announcements
Engraved in gold

But all across the country
Choking with oppression
On subway trains
And corners
In tenements
And jail cells
After Hearing you were here
Black faces
Smiled tender, thoughtful smiles
Black hands
Slapped five
Black hearts
Beat songs of freedom
And welcomed to the family
A new Black hope

Assata Shakur

To all the press, she was the reigning queen
    Of what reporters called the BLA,
Whose phantom face was regularly seen
    From Harlem's hills to San Francisco Bay.
Indicted for a host of major crimes,
    From murder to the robbery of vaults,
She went to trial so many different times
    To be convicted once for others' faults.
Her child was born behind the prison gate,
    The product of a moment's stolen grace;
Her poems were spun from pangs of love and hate,
    Admixed with yearnings for a freer space.
Her lawyers worked their fingers to the bone
    But she did better still upon her own.

Law Enforcement

Government-created crime has become an all too familiar phenomenon of the past decade or so. The first such endeavor to gain widespread public recognition was, of course, Abscam, in which one United States Senator and seven Representatives were the prime targets. With Melvin Weinberg, a convicted swindler, making the initial contacts, FBI agents, masquerading as Middle Eastern sheiks, replete with plush yachts, fashionable townhouses, and phony business fronts, offered substantial bribes to the legislators in return for promised favors.

In Frontload, another FBI operation, Norman Howard, a white-collar criminal with an extensive record, who played much the same role as did Weinberg in Abscam, was used by the FBI in connection with the investigation of organized crime figures in federally financed construction projects in New York and New Jersey. The scenario called for Howard to act as the representative of a legitimate insurance company, capable of writing bids, payment, and performance bonds for construction projects. Equipped with a corporate seal and all the necessary forms, he wrote many millions of dollars in performance bonds, which enabled the companies under scrutiny to bid successfully on a number of such projects. Not only did the issuance of these bonds make a number of serious crimes possible, but it resulted in lawsuits totalling some $343,000,000 against the U.S. Government. Parenthetically, Howard, who absconded with an estimated $1,000,000 in premiums he had collected, apparently will never be prosecuted for his theft.

Buyin involved an FBI undercover agent posing as the employee of a California-based company which wished to invest in a Washington state gambling enterprise with the understanding that casino gambling and slot machines would soon be legalized. The agent finally met a gambling lobbyist who said that he could introduce him to the Speaker of the House and the Senate Majority Leader in the Washington legislature. The lobbyist said that he was sure that both solons would be willing to introduce and support the desired bill, provided they were adequately compensated for their efforts. Thousands of dollars were paid out by the

Bureau to the lobbyist as a "consulting fee" and to the Speaker as "a campaign contribution" to further this project, despite the fact that the charges against the primary target, a local official, "were never proven."

Labou concerned an investigation into bid-rigging, bond irregularities and other aspects of alleged construction fraud in the Washington, D.C. vicinity. Here the FBI went into the construction business, renting offices and renovating two houses in Washington in what it termed "an elaborate facade [for] the most complex and expensive operation in our history." It first utilized an independent businessman to run the construction company, but when he proved unable to obtain bonding on a short-term basis, it became, first, a coindemnitor of all awarded projects, and then, full owner of the organization which eventually completed four major construction jobs. Ironically, one of the two houses renovated in connection with this operation became the meeting place of many of the Abscam subjects.

The viability of all such sting operations depends entirely upon the constantly narrowing judicial approach to the affirmative defense of entrapment. Almost thirty years ago the Supreme Court held that "the fact that the government agents merely afford opportunities or facilities for the commission of the offense does not constitute entrapment. Entrapment occurs only when the criminal conduct was the product of the creative activity of law enforcement officials." Fifteen years later the Court stated that the entrapment defense "focuses on the intent or predisposition of the defendant to commit the crime rather than the conduct of the Government's agent." The test approved by its majority for determining such "intent or predisposition" is, unfortunately, a highly subjective one, permitting what one dissenting justice called "hearsay, suspicion and rumor" to be put before the jury by the prosecution.

In the DeLorean cocaine case at least one jury adopted the viewpoint of the overwhelming majority of informed commentators, including the prestigious American Law Institute, that the only proper inquiry is the extent of government misconduct rather than the subjective inclinations of any particular sting's quarries. Put another way by a dissenting Supreme Court Justice in 1977:

If involvement in [a criminal enterprise] is of a kind that could induce or instigate the commission of a crime by one not ready and willing to commit it, then—regardless of the character or propensities of the particular person induced—I think entrapment has occurred. For in that situation, the Government has engaged in the impermissible manufacturing of crime, and the federal courts should bar the prosecution in order to preserve the institutional integrity of the system of federal criminal justice. . . .

Law Enforcement

The crime's conceived by some official state,
    With each ingredient supplied with care,
Down to the type of most enticing bait
    And who'll do what to whom and when and where.
When all the actors are in proper place
    And everyone acquainted with his role,
The sting is blessed with governmental grace
    As hidden cameras begin to roll.
The bribes are hung before the victim's eyes
    By agents hidden in exotic clothes,
Or erstwhile thieves who, to their great surprise,
    Are now the partners of their former foes.
Without a clue to guide one where to look,
    It's hard to tell the policeman from the crook.

William Worthy

In 1956, William Worthy, a black reporter for the *Baltimore Afro-American*, went to what was then referred to as Red China, in violation of a restriction against such travel in his passport. When he returned to the United States, his passport was seized by immigration authorities, and I was retained by the American Civil Liberties Union to attempt to get it back. Although I was initially unsuccessful, Worthy managed to travel around the world for years with nothing more than an affidavit of identity.

Some years later he voyaged to Cuba,—then, as now, off limits for most American citizens. Upon his return he was arrested at the Miami International Airport, and charged under an obscure statute making it a crime for anyone who had violated passport restrictions to return to the United States. Although he was found guilty in the trial court, a higher court reversed his conviction on the ground that no one could be legitimately prosecuted for coming home. The court's words deserve repetition now:

We are not unaware of the reluctance with which courts should reach decisions declaring enactments of Congress to be unconstitutional. We realize, though, the duty resting upon the judiciary to protect the citizen in the exercise of the fundamental rights which the fundamental law has conferred upon him. In the performance of that duty, and for the reasons which we have attempted to state, it is our conclusion that the Government cannot say to its citizen, standing beyond its border, that his reentry into the land of his allegiance is a criminal offense; and this we conclude is a sound principle whether or not the citizen has a passport, and however wrongful may have been his conduct in effecting his departure.

William Worthy

The State Department said we couldn't go
    To Cuba, China, and North Vietnam,
Because, it said, to interrupt the flow
    Of travelers would hurt each reddish land.
One writer thought such curbs would bar the news
    And entered China's mainland to observe
What lay behind the Silken Curtain's hues
    And lost his passport for his lawless verve.
He decided that it was Cuba's turn
    And sought one more forbidden fleece.
No sooner had he made his safe return,
    He was arrested by his country's police.
They censured him when he began to roam,
    Then charged him with the crime of coming home.

My Brother's Death

As I was preparing this book for publication, my brother Michael suddenly died. He and I had started a law partnership shortly after our graduation from Columbia Law School and remained together until my involvement in civil rights litigation became so intense that I could no longer shoulder my responsibilities in our firm. Michael was always sympathetic to the fact that my interest in the regular practice of law diminished sharply after 1961, and he saw to it that I received the same draw as he did—even though I was no longer working on paying cases—until we parted company in 1970, after the conclusion of the Chicago Conspiracy Trial. We were different in every imaginable way but one—we loved and respected each other.

My Brother's Death

He died in springtime, full against the grain
    Of what was happening in every tree,
This man with whom I lived through childhood's reign
    In that forgotten world of infancy.
So different from each other though we shared
    The common chromosomes of mutual birth,
Yet we began our days uniquely paired
    To walk together upon the waiting earth.
Somewhere along the path, the trail had split
    And sent us spinning off on different ways
With only fantasies of lamps unlit
    To kindle shadowed hints of former days.
The past receded far beyond recall,
    But in the end it mattered not at all.

Foreign Policy

Since World War II it has been an integral element of American foreign policy to cozy up to any anti-Soviet right-wing dictator. Spain's Franco, Portugal's Salazar, the Dominican Republic's Trujillo, the Shah of Iran, Chile's Pinochet, and Paraguay's Stroessner, the Duvaliers, father and son, in Haiti, the Somozas of Nicaragua, the Philippines' Marcos, and the pre-Falkland Islands Argentine junta—are some prime examples. This fact of international politics is probably best epitomized by Franklin Delano Roosevelt's reputed remark in 1936 to the State Department's Sumner Welles about the first Somoza, "He's a son of a bitch, but he's our son of a bitch."

Foreign Policy

The death squads in El Salvador are fine,
    Except when they assassinate our nuns;
We loved the junta in the Argentine
    And sold the Shah his tanks and planes and guns.
We cozy up to Stroessner's Paraguay,
    For Marcos and the Turks, we beat the band;
There's no one friendlier than Pinochet
    While Guatemala earns our helping hand.
We always got along with Papa Doc,
    Somoza and Battista on our side,
Taught Uruguay how to get out of hock
    And looked the other way at apartheid.
There's lots of room in Uncle's ample bed
    For any realm that swears it's anti-Red.

Judges Are Made

The Constitution gives Presidents the power to nominate all federal judges who must then be approved by a majority of the Senate. However, with some notable exceptions, the latter body has always approved the chief executive's choices. Since the federal judiciary enjoys lifetime tenure, the selection of its members tends to perpetuate the political philosophies of their nominators. John Adams took advantage of this fact of life by filling a number of court vacancies on the eve of Jefferson's inauguration with the so-called "midnight judges" in the hope that they would keep Federalist principles alive and well during the ensuing Republican administration.

During the 1984 Presidential campaign, the Democrats made much of the fact that, given the advanced ages of many members of the Supreme Court, it was extremely likely that some vacancies would occur during the next four years. They maintained that their candidate could be expected to name far better qualified jurists than would Ronald Reagan. To counter this argument, Justice William H. E. Rehnquist, the ideological leader of the Court's conservative majority, tried to assure the electorate that no President could control the decisions of any nominee once the latter had been confirmed by the Senate. However, given the President's appointment of Justice O'Connor and many of his choices for the lower federal courts, the High Court will most surely reflect his own antediluvian social, economic, and political theories.

Judges Are Made

The President selects the judges who
    He's sure must share his ideology
And see the law from his own point of view
    As a device to roll back liberty.
He searches for the ideal candidate
    Who's willing to destroy the age-old wall
That lies between religion and the state
    By letting pupils pray at morning call.
The persons who obtain his regal nod
    Are those to whom abortion holds no sway,
Who think that it is highly anti-God
    To fight a creche upon the public way.
Long after Mr. Reagan leaves the throne,
    Each district will contain at least one clone.

Medgar Evers

Medgar Evers was the NAACP field secretary in Mississippi when I first met him on a plane bound for that state in the fall of 1961. I was on my way to defend the Freedom Riders, who had been arrested for riding integrated buses into Jackson earlier that year. My attention was drawn to him by the NAACP button on his lapel. I quickly introduced myself, and we talked about our common interests until we landed an hour or so later.

He was intensely interested in registering black voters in the Magnolia State, and his success in this area undoubtedly led to his assassination on June 12, 1963. A sniper, hidden in the bushes across the road from his house, shot him as he was walking up the steps of his home returning from an organizational meeting. His funeral, three days later, which was attended by Roy Wilkins, Ralph Bunche, Martin Luther King, Jr., and many other civil rights activitists, almost resulted in a massive confrontation between the mourners and the Jackson police. The timely intervention of John Doar of the Justice Department's Civil Rights Division, who stood between the two advancing forces, succeeded in defusing the impending conflict and surely prevented an additional, and probably greater, tragedy.

Many years later I was one of the attorneys for the students of Medgar Evers College in Brooklyn, New York, who had occupied the president's office as a protest against what they considered to be his repressive administration. When an enlightened judge permitted the sit-in to continue under certain conditions, which were met, I thought that Medgar would certainly have been more than proud of all concerned. Shortly thereafter, the president resigned, and the college today has a new, and I hope, a more responsive administration; however, there are some ominous signs that such may not be the case.

Medgar Evers

We met aboard a plane so long ago,
    En route to murder and magnolia trees,
Two men from worlds as varied as we know
    Whose lives would touch like petals in the breeze.
The outpost of the NAACP,
    He roamed the fearsome Mississippi land,
Exhorting those who were not truly free
    To break their shackles' last remaining strand.
The murderer, recalling Emmett Till,
    Who died for whistling at a distaff white,
Was crouched nearby and savoring for the kill
    That would, he thought, turn back the racial blight.
That he was wrong the future was to say—
    The time had passed for fear to block the way.

Mississippi Summer

On Monday, June 22, more than twenty years ago, I received an early morning call from Nathan Schwerner of Pelham, New York. He said, "My son, Mickey, and two other young civil right workers are missing in Mississippi. They left Meridian in Mickey's car yesterday morning for a trip to Neshoba County, and they have not returned or called in. Can you find out for me where they are— my wife and I are worried sick."

As one of the lawyers for the Council of Federated Organizations (COFO), a loose coalition of civil rights groups that had recruited some 1,000 student volunteers, including my eldest daughter, I immediately contacted the Neshoba County Sheriff's Office in Philadelphia, Mississippi. Mickey, who with his wife ran a Meridian biracial community center for the Congress of Racial Equality, was accompanied by Andrew Goodman, a white anthropology major from Queens College, New York, and a local black plasterer, James E. Chaney. A drawling voice informed me that Mickey and his two companions had been arrested by a deputy the previous evening. The three youths, part of COFO's advance party, had been picked up for driving sixty-five miles per hour in a thirty-mile speed zone and held at the county jail "for investigation" until 10:30 P.M.. Chaney, who had been driving Schwerner's late-model Ford station wagon, paid a $20 fine, and they were finally released. They had last been seen leaving town on State Highway 19.

When I reached Bob Moses, COFO's director, he told me that Schwerner and his two friends had left that city at 9:30 A.M. on June 21 to inspect the damage done to the Mount Zion Methodist Church. The hub of civil rights activities in Neshoba County, the church had been mysteriously set afire a week earlier. Although all of COFO's personnel had been directed to report their whereabouts regularly whenever they left their home bases, Moses told me no calls had been received from the missing trio after their departure from Meridian.

Later that day Deputy Sheriff Cecil Ray Price, who had arrested the three, said that after their release, he had ordered them "to leave the county." Sheriff Lawrence A. Rainey, a burly, tobacco-chewing man, told a newspaper reporter that "if they're missing, they just hid somewhere, trying to get a lot of publicity out of it, I figure." A year later both officials, along with sixteen other defendants, would be indicted by a federal Grand Jury, and charged with conspiracy to intercept and kill Schwerner, Goodman, and Chaney.

The next day the burned-out station wagon was found in a swamp on Bogue Chitto Creek, fifteen miles northeast of Philadelphia and some fifty feet off State Highway 21. In ensuing weeks a nationwide search for the three men was conducted. On August 4, after paying $25,000 for a tip from an informer, the FBI found the bodies of the civil rights workers, buried fifteen feet apart, under a newly erected earthen cattle pond dam in a thickly wooded area six miles southwest of Philadelphia. Each had been shot to death.

Before COFO's "Mississippi Summer" ended, some 60,000 new black registrants had been added to the voting rolls. This accomplishment, won at such cost, prompted enactment of the Voting Rights Act of 1965, legislation that eventually altered forever the balance of political power in the South. Within one year after its passage the number of blacks registered in Mississippi and four other southern states had increased by almost 50 percent. Of equal significance, it provided the foundation for the Presidential campaign, two decades later, of the Rev. Jesse Jackson.

Mickey Schwerner, Andy Goodman, and Jim Chaney may have died on a back road in pain and terror, but not in vain.

At summer's end, COFO's student volunteers returned to their campuses with the sure knowledge that they had indeed wrought a major miracle. The murders of their comrades had shocked and terrified most of them, as well as their worried parents, but they had worked on and hoped for the best, somehow sublimating their fears of the worst. That they kept on was undoubtedly because their slain friends had become for them, as Rabbi Arthur J. Lelyveld had put it at Andy Goodman's memorial service on August 10, 1964: "the eternal evocation of all the hosts of beautiful young men and women who are carrying forth the struggle for which they gave their lives."

Mississippi Summer

They had no thought in mind except to try
    To change the world in one short season's flight;
They did not think that they would ever die
    For doing what their instincts said was right.
They perished on a backwoods country lane,
    These integrated victims of the past,
The bullets that destroyed each youthful brain
    Were meant to make a dying system last.
Their bodies lay, just fifteen feet apart,
    Beneath an earthen dam for forty days,
Until a bonus bought a change of heart
    In one who knew their killer's hidden ways.
At summer's end their comrades left the field
    With sixty thousand registrants their yield.

Jane Fonda

No one can gainsay that Jane Fonda was a courageous and out-spoken opponent of the Vietnamese conflict. At the risk of her burgeoning career in an industry which is notoriously skittish about controversial film stars, she perservered in her determination to do what she could, including traveling to Hanoi, to stop what she considered to be the immoral and illegal use of American troops in Southeast Asia. I ran into her on many occasions in various parts of the country where she exhorted student and other audiences to take a vigorous propeace stand.

To some degree she has continued her political activities by participating in antinuclear demonstrations. But she has seemed far more interested in making money than remaining on the firing line. In particular, her enormously successful women's exercise workout book and record have changed her image from that of a militant crusader for human rights to that of a highly paid gym instructor.

Jane Fonda

An actress at the start of her career,
　　She dared to jeopardize her upward climb
By thundering to all who cared to hear
　　Her opposition to her country's crime.
There was no role she played with fiercer pride
　　Than that of critic of a dirty war;
She sought to interrupt the bloody tide
　　That stained our honor with its endless gore.
On college campuses throughout the land,
　　She brought her glamor to the side of right;
She understood that fame had its demand
　　To justify the shining of the light.
Strange that this voice that once mouthed urgent pleas
　　Now teaches women how to bend their knees.

Exclusionary Rule

One of the chief causes of the discontent that led to the American Revolution was the hated Writs of Assistance issued by the Crown. These documents gave their recipients virtually perpetual power to search any ship or building and seize any property claimed to be contraband. The abuse of these writs, particularly in Massachusetts, was a constant source of irritation to the colonists. The Fourth Amendment to the Constitution, with its emphasis on "the right of the people to be secure in their persons, houses, papers and effects, against unreasonable searches and seizures" was a direct result of this reaction.

With this in view the Supreme Court, for almost a century, has held that illegally seized evidence may not be introduced by the prosecution in criminal trials. In 1984, this exclusionary rule, as it came to be known, was seriously undermined by the Court's ultraconservative majority, which authorized the use of such evidence if the officer seizing it thought that he was acting legally in so doing. This so-called "good faith exception" now opens the way for the wholesale destruction of the exclusionary rule by encouraging official misconduct and perjury.

Exclusionary Rule

The colonists made one thing crystal clear—
    They could not stand their king's propensity,
By use of force or subterfuge or fear,
    To search their homes or seize their property.
By declaration and amendment plain,
    They tried to end the evils of their age
So that no one could weld the broken chain
    Or reconstruct once more the shattered cage.
The Court's majority now sanctifies
    Whatever violations come to light,
Provided only that the policeman cries
    That he believed that what he did was right.
How gleeful must be George's restless shade,
    Now that we have exhumed his stock in trade.

Iran

When the ailing Shah of Iran, faced with imminent revolution, fled his country in early 1979, he eventually sought refuge in the United States, where he hoped to obtain needed medical treatment for advanced cancer of the lymph nodes. After being urged to do so by David Rockefeller, Chairman of the Board of the Chase Manhattan Bank, and ex-Secretary of State Henry Kissinger, President Carter agreed, in the fall of 1979, to permit the former monarch to enter the Cornell-New York Hospital Center. No sooner had he done so than enraged Iranian students retaliated by seizing and occupying the American Embassy in Teheran, as well as capturing some sixty Americans employed or assigned there, and holding them hostage for what was to amount to 444 days. To many political observers the way in which Carter met this crisis in international relations was primarily responsible for his 1980 defeat by Ronald Reagan.

Shortly after the seizure of the hostages, I was asked by members of the Iranian Embassy to come to Washington to discuss ways in which to end the impasse. I did so, but as events later proved, private legal advice played little if any role in the eventual resolution of the situation.

Iran

The revolution in Iran had made
    The Shah a man without a native land,
Condemned to wander, ailing and afraid,
    To any place his person was not banned.
The Peacock Tsar, a prime depositor
    Of Rockefeller's Chase Manhattan Bank,
Strove for the right to travel to this shore
    By pulling on his monetary rank.
While doctors vied to treat his royal disease,
    His former subjects wanted him returned,
So that they'd have a chance to judge his pleas
    To charges that they thought he'd more than earned.
The President gave in to power's sway
    And sacrificed his embassy away.

Alfred Griffin

In mid-1983, the President decided to send American Marines to battle-torn Beirut to serve as a "peacekeeping force." Accordingly, units at Camp LeJeune, North Carolina, the home base of the Second Marine Amphibious Unit, were alerted for imminent departure to Lebanon. Their training, however, included substantial combat orientation, more conducive to a military offensive than to the requirements of a peacekeeping mission.

One black Marine, Corporal Alfred Griffin, a Muslim from his earliest days, felt that the tenets of his religion forbade his participation in offensive warfare. Because of his strong religious sentiments, Corporal Griffin, the leader of a machine gun squad, deliberately missed his unit's movement and went AWOL. When he returned to his base a few days later, he was informed that his company had been diverted to the invasion of Grenada and, if he would rejoin it, he would not be court-martialed. Feeling the same scruples about Grenada as he did about Lebanon, Corporal Griffin refused the offer.

Along with Randy Scott-McLaughlin and Ron Kuby, I represented him at the ensuing court-martial where we were thwarted in our efforts to present witnesses prepared to testify about the right of members of the armed forces to refuse to obey what they considered to be illegal orders, the so-called Nuremberg defense. However, we were permitted to call two Muslim ministers (*Imams*) who stated that the Koran forbids its believers to engage in offensive warfare. Despite this testimony Griffin was convicted and sentenced to reduction in rank, forfeiture of pay, a bad conduct discharge, and four months' confinement at hard labor. Three months later, he was released from the Camp Lejeune brig and is presently appealing the refusal of the military judge to permit a Nuremberg-type defense.

Alfred Griffin

The President announced that he would send
    Marines to Lebanon to keep the peace,
So that a brutal civil war would end
    And years of Arab-Christian killings cease.
In fact, the purpose of this sudden plan
    Was to support one of the warring sides,
And stateside training given to each man
    Stressed combat rather than defensive strides.
One soldier felt aggressive war to be
    A sin against the Koran's sacred laws
And missed his unit's movement to the sea
    In deference to a more exalted cause.
It took more bravery to utter 'no'
    Than join his acquiescent friends and go.

Reprieve

All lawyers who have handled death penalty prosecutions know the agony of waiting for a court to grant a stay of execution. With my perennial colleague, Arthur Kinoy, I went through this torment in *Commonwealth* v. *Thomas Carlton Wansley*, a case involving a sixteen-year-old black resident of Lynchburg, Virginia, who had been convicted of raping a white woman in that city in 1966. When the stay was finally granted, shortly before Wansley's scheduled execution date, our feeling of overwhelming relief was only secondary to that which must have been experienced by our Death Row client. Fortunately, his conviction was eventually reversed and, after several years of legal maneuvering, he was finally released. "Gruesome Gertie" is the name colloquially applied to Louisiana's overactive electric chair.

Reprieve

The execution warrant had been signed
　　And Gruesome Gertie's wiring checked through;
The governor states he will not change his mind,
　　The doomed man gives his final interview.
A lawyer stands, a hundred miles away,
　　Before three judges of the Circuit Court,
And pleads for just another brief delay
　　While pointing out that time is very short.
The priest, accompanied by his breviary,
　　Stands waiting patiently beside the door
That opens wide upon eternity,
　　And murmurs prayers along the corridor.
Sweet Christ, the blessed telephone rings out,
　　The triumph of the grave is still in doubt.

Lie Detector

All societies have attempted, throughout recorded time, to find a relatively reliable method to isolate truth in human affairs. At first a solemn oath was thought to insure that its taker would not deviate from the straight and narrow. Then, as the fear of hell and damnation began to diminish, our ancestors resorted to such tactics as the prolonged dunking in water of those suspected of crime or forcing them to hold hot coals in their hands. If the defendant was drowned or was burnt, he or she must have been lying; if not, truth had been revealed. Another method was to have champions for both the accused and accuser fight to the death—the side whose gladiator was victorious was judged to be the truthful one.

As the age of superstition waned, people began to resort to jury trials and, in particular, cross-examination, to ferret out the wheat from the chaff. In this century of mechanization the invention of the lie detector has raised the issue of the ability of a machine to tell whether a subject is lying or not. Most courts have refused to permit the results of lie detector tests to be introduced in evidence, claiming that it is not yet sufficiently reliable; but, given our growing faith in mechanical devices, it is probably only a matter of time before it gains universal approval.

Lie Detector

The ancients had a unique way to learn
    The innocence of those accused of crime—
Their hands held in the flames would never burn
    Or they could live submerged for any time.
Another method was to hire one
    To struggle with the champion of the state,
And then determine that, whoever won,
    The victor's party must the truth relate.
This type of trial by combat or ordeal
    Was finally replaced by jural guess
As to which version of the facts was real
    And whose escutcheon Providence should bless.
They tell us now that tubes and colored wires
    Can separate the honest from the liars.

Birmingham

Martin Luther King frequently referred to Birmingham, Alabama, as Bombingham, because of the great number of unsolved explosions, many of a suspected racial nature, that took place in that city in the fifties and sixties. Perhaps the most heinous of these occurred on a Sunday morning in the fall of 1963, at the Fifth Avenue Baptist Church, which had been a staging area for Dr. King's protest demonstrations four months earlier. Just before worship services that day, a tremendous explosion ripped through the church's basement where its Sunday School classrooms were located. When the smoke cleared, the bodies of four young girls, dressed in their Sunday best, were discovered in the rubble.

Birmingham

They call the city Pittsburgh southern style
    Because it tapped the wealth that steel could bring,
But it was known once, for a tragic while,
    As Bombingham where dynamite was king.
The night before the Sunday worship call,
    A bomb was planted by some vengeful men
Behind the church's unprotected wall,
    Its timer set to detonate at ten.
The deadly clock ticked on relentlessly
    As children hurried on their basement way,
With no idea that some would never see
    Another hour of another day.
To honor segregation's dying breath,
    Four barely started lives were blown to death.

146

Emmet Till

In 1955, fourteen-year-old Emmet Till, a black Chicago youth, was sent by his parents to spend the summer with relatives in Greenwood, Mississippi. When he dared to whistle at a passing white woman, he was dragged from his house by three men who murdered him and threw his body into a nearby creek. When his killers were quickly acquitted by an all-white state jury, and a federal grand jury refused to indict them, the case became a rallying cry for civil rights activists the country over. This tragic case was very much in my mind when I began to assemble the available facts in the shooting on December 22, 1984, of four black youths on a New York City subway train by Bernhard Hugo Goetz, particularly when a hastily convened grand jury refused to indict him for anything but illegal gun possession. As one of the attorneys for Darrell Cabey, the most seriously injured of Mr. Goetz's targets, I was appalled, not only by the cold and calculated nature of the shootings themselves, but by the initial cavalcade of public and media support for an emotionally disturbed would-be murderer. Fortunately, a significant change in public opinion took place when it was revealed the Goetz had, after examining the bodies of his fallen victims, decided that Cabey didn't "look too bad," and shot him again, severing the spine with a dum dum bullet. A new grand jury then returned indictments charging the so-called "Subway Vigilante" with four counts of attempted murder.

Emmet Till

Perhaps it was a dare from friends at play,
    Or just a youthful whim that mastered fear—
When Emmet saw the woman pass his way,
    He pursed his lips and whistled long and clear.
The sound reverberated through the air,
    And shocked surprise soon turned to bitter hate,
As whites assembled near the village square
    To reach consensus on the culprit's fate.
It took a moment for the bold to cry
    That, for his sneer at crinoline and lace,
This fourteen-year-old black boy had to die
    To keep the local nigras in their place.
In order to make sure that he was truly dead,
    They crushed his skull and shot him through the head.

Augusto César Sandino

On the day before Christmas in 1926, United States Marines invaded Nicaragua in order to abort a popular rebellion against a Washington-supported puppet government. This marked the second time that the country had been occupied by American forces, the first having taken place fourteen years earlier under similar circumstances. The new invasion was, according to the State Department, justified by requests from unnamed sources for the protection of American property interests. President Coolidge put it more bluntly two weeks later when he told the Congress that: "The United States cannot . . . fail to view with deep concern any serious threat to stability and constitutional government in Nicaragua leading toward anarchy and jeopardizing American interests. . . . It has always been and remains [our] policy in such circumstances to take the steps necessary for the preservation of the lives, property, and the interests of its citizens and the government itself."

Augusto Nicolás Calderón Sandino, who was then working for an oil company in Mexico, was so affronted by the landing of the Marines, that he took his life savings and returned to his native Nicaragua and, in his own words, "got into active political life." With a handful of followers, armed with a few weapons purchased in Honduras, Sandino resolved to rid his country of its American occupiers. Starting in the rugged mountain area of Las Segovias, the original Sandinista army of twenty-nine men soon swelled to three hundred, and succeeded in liberating village after village. For seven long years he managed to keep his army intact, despite all efforts by the Marines to destroy it and, in the process, became a folk hero throughout all of Latin America.

At last, in December of 1932, primarily because of the successes of Sandino's troops, the American forces began leaving Nicaragua. However, Anastasio Somoza, the commander of the country's US-sponsored National Guard, who was to assume dictatorial powers on the first day of 1937, had Sandino and two of his chief lieutenants shot to death late on the evening of February 21, 1923 while they were in Managua for negotiations at the invitation of the government. Just before a bullet shattered his brain, Sandino was heard to say, "My political leaders have played jokes with me."

Forty-seven years later another guerrilla army, with Sandino's name on its lips, drove Somoza's son from power and completed *El Generale*'s work. Today, following Ronald Reagan's reelection, the country lives in daily dread of a third American invasion.

Augusto César Sandino

His army numbered only twenty-nine
　　When he began to struggle to breathe free,
But grew apace until his ragged line
　　Patrolled from Las Segovias to the sea.
His country occupied by Washington,
　　He sought a refuge in a mountain height,
And taught his *campesinos* when to run
　　Away from harm and when to stand and fight.
For seven years his phantom soldiers bled
　　To drive the gringos from their fatherland,
Until, at last, Somoza shot him dead
　　With final victory so near at hand.
Despite the years, a bullet in the brain,
　　Today, *El Generale* rides again.

Judas Goat

A judas goat is one who betrays his fellows by leading them to the slaughterhouse, thereby saving his own life. In the Julius and Ethel Rosenberg case the government saw to it that all of the major members of the prosecution staff as well as the trial judge were Jewish. Long after the trial it was revealed, through FBI documents, that the latter, Irving R. Kaufman, had not only agreed before the trial to impose the death penalty in the event of convictions, but had sought to impede the couple's appeals and, long after they were executed, to inhibit critics of his role in the case.

Judas Goat

The youthful judge, who'd sat for just a while,
    Was chosen by the state to try the pair,
And promised that, if guilt came after trial,
    He'd sentence each defendant to the chair.
Before his judgment was announced, he lied
    That he had not consulted anyone,
Although he understood deep down inside
    That he had talked at length with Washington.
When he finished with his sentence dread,
    He tried to sabotage each new appeal,
And even after they were long since dead,
    He sought revenge on critics of his zeal.
He can't forget, however he may try,
    That he condemned the Rosenbergs to die.

The Law of Libel

In a landmark decision in 1964, the Supreme Court reversed a $500,000 judgment obtained by the police commissioner of Montgomery, Alabama, in a libel suit against the *New York Times* and a number of black clergymen. The latter had signed a full-page advertisement in the *Times*, charging that there existed "an unprecedented wave of terror" against blacks engaged in nonviolent demonstrations in the South. In essence, the suit had charged that the advertisement in question contained a number of inaccuracies such as that Martin Luther King, Jr. had been arrested seven times during such demonstrations when, in fact, he had been arrested only four times.

In reversing the judgment, the Court stated that it was taking into consideration a "background of a profound national commitment to the principle that debate on public issues would be uninhibited, robust, and wide-open, and it may well include vehement, caustic, and sometimes unpleasantly sharp attacks on government and public officials." It then laid down as a rule of constitutional law that public officials, even when falsely disparaged, could only recover damages when they could prove that "the statement was made with actual malice"—that is, with knowledge that it was false or with reckless disregard of whether it was false or not.

While I share the feelings of the late Supreme Court Justices Black and Douglas that all defamation suits inhibit free speech and should be prohibited, I agree that public figures must at least prove that false statements concerning them were uttered maliciously before they can win any damages. That juries take this legal requirement seriously was amply demonstrated in former Israeli Defense Minister Ariel Sharon's recently concluded libel action against *Time* magazine. His panel found that he had been falsely accused of some responsibility for the 1982 massacre of Palestinian civilians by Christian Phalangists at two refugee camps on the outskirts of Beirut, but refused to award him any money because no malice on the magazine's part had been shown. A short time later, General William C. Westmoreland, despairing of being able to prove malicious intent, voluntarily discontinued his suit against the Columbia Broadcasting System for reporting that he had deliberately downgraded reports of enemy troop strength in Vietnam in order to deceive President Lyndon B. Johnson.

The Law of Libel

It used to be that if they called you Red
    Or wrote that you were just a little gay,
You'd hurry into court and sue them dead
    And try to take their bank account away.
But now it's very difficult to win
    If you are someone in the public eye,
For you must prove that they had done you in
    With malice motivating every lie.
It's open season to malign the great,
    So long as you can piously proclaim
That you believe the truth of what you state
    And that there was no motive to defame.
In other words, be sure that you annoy
    Those only who are not the hoi polloi.

Greenham Common Women

Greenham Common, a plain which comprises hundreds of acres about sixty miles west of London, was leased to the United States Air Force as a base in 1951. Thirty years later forty protestors against the siting of close to a hundred cruise missiles at the base marched from Cardiff, Wales, to the Common. Although their trek received little publicity, it eventually galvanized the establishment of a peace camp outside of the main gates. Since its founding, women from the camp have engaged in all forms of protest activities ranging from a symbolic "embracing" of the base to taking over a sentry box or cutting down a mile of fence. Only recently, hundreds and thousands of demonstrators, both at the camp and around the world, have joined in various protest activities on the occasion of NATO's largest war games since World War II.

The Greenham Common Women

They understood the madness of this world
    And vowed that sanity would be restored
Before the damning thunderbolts were hurled
    Upon the biding universal horde.
The globe is mined with secret missile sites,
    Computerized to decimate the foe;
The people dream of radiated nights,
    Illuminated by atomic glow.
The women sense the holocaust is near,
    But hope they can avert the deadly trend;
They know the threat will never disappear
    Until the human spirit wills its end.
While old men hide their guided toys of death,
    The rest of us stand by and hold our breath.

The Police

Over the years I have had many contacts with both federal and state law enforcement officers throughout the country. A few have attacked me physically—in such places as St. Augustine, Florida and Brooklyn, New York—while many have done so verbally, particularly in those cases where people I represented were charged with crimes of violence against their colleagues. In the beginning I accepted the epithet "pigs" applied to the police by many of my clients but as time went by I realized that these agencies were far from monolithic and that their members, in doing their communities' dirty work, ranged all over the qualitative scale of human worth.

Recently, I have been asked, to my great surprise, to speak at several New York City precincts, and my audiences reflected these varied reactions. To some I was nothing more than a perennial defender of "cop killers," while others saw me as someone who played a necessary role in the criminal justice system. In between, the appraisals covered a wide spectrum of likes and dislikes, usually generated by profound misconceptions of lawyers like myself.

The fact remains that a significant number of officers, usually white, place an extremely low value on the lives of Third World people, a state of being which has resulted in hundreds of unnecessary deaths and contributed heavily to racial unrest in many urban centers. In a supposedly maturing society it is high time that police officers, as well as the rest of us, understand that .38-caliber bullets simply cannot remain the determinative element as to who lives and who dies. When that occurs, we will have crossed—assuming that we have not all been atomized—a welcome threshold.

The Police

There are two police departments, people say,
    The one composed of psychopaths quite mad,
The other visioned by the PBA,
    Staffed with facsimiles of Galahad.
The graves are filled with bodies of the dead,
    The victims of a tragic point of view
That makes a difference in the use of lead
    To keep the status quo both safe and true.
Yet on the other hand, we know full well
    To think in monolithic terms is mean
And that there is no heaven nor no hell,
    But only neutral acres in between.
The truth, it seems, is very hard to find
    But those who yield to mania over mind.

The Bradens

In the spring of 1954, Carl and Anne Braden, white residents of Louisville, Kentucky, bought a home in a segregated suburb and promptly transferred it to Andrew and Charlotte Wade, a black couple. As soon as the Wades moved in, a cross was burned on their lawn, guns were fired into the house, and rocks were thrown through the windows. Six weeks later a dynamite bomb, which had been placed under their child's bedroom, exploded and destroyed half of the house. Fortunately, the house was empty at the time and there were no injuries.

No one was ever charged with the crime, but the Bradens and five of their friends were eventually indicted for conspiring to overthrow the government of the State of Kentucky because of their efforts in behalf of the Wades. Carl Braden, the only defendant to be tried, was convicted and sentenced to fifteen years in prison and a fine of $5,000. Three years later Kentucky's highest court reversed the conviction on the grounds that the state's sedition statute could not be used against Braden.

In 1968, when the Bradens were once more charged with sedition for their organizing activities in rural Pike County, Kentucky, I was one of the lawyers who persuaded a three-judge federal court to declare the statute unconstitutional.

The Bradens

For Carl and Anne, the message was quite clear—
    They would not compromise their moral code,
No matter how much misery or fear
    It cost to travel on the higher road.
They found a house whose owner wished to sell
    And signed the contract as any buyers would,
So that a nonwhite family could dwell
    In Louisville's Caucasian neighborhood.
This sin against the mores of their times
    Subjected them to swift official hate
And they were charged with varied heinous crimes
    Like threatening to overthrow the state.
But in the end Kentucky's people heard
    That courage was much more than just a word.

Object Lesson

When I attended law school, there were only three women in a class of nearly 200. Now the number of female students studying law has reached substantial proportions, with some schools reporting nearly fifty percent in their entering classes. Because of this, women lawyers have become commonplace in the trial courts, and many are now sitting on both state and federal benches.

Despite this steady trend many male attorneys and judges still maintain the same chauvinistic attitudes that characterized their relationships with the women who began to invade their exclusive provinces in the middle of the 1960s. The event depicted in this sonnet is a poetic version of what I witnessed in a New York courtroom several years ago. It brought home to me, as well as to the judge involved, that we now have a unisex bar where the old male-female dichotomy can no longer exist unchallenged.

Object Lesson

It was a fairly routine day in court
    When *People versus Brown* was called to trial.
The judge, a squat and rotund clubhouse sort,
    Gave each attorney a most glowing smile.
"It's nice to see a pretty face," he said
    To the young lawyer for the accused,
And then turned brighter than the brightest red
    To realize that she was not amused.
"I may not have your gender's point of view,"
    She snapped, "nor know as much about the lex;
But I expect to be addressed by you
    Without the condescension of your sex."
In one brief flash, his Honor knew at last
    The ancient ways were relics of the past.

Kathy Boudin

In March of 1970, a townhouse in New York's Greenwich Village was destroyed by an explosion attributed to the making of bombs in its basement by former members of Students for a Democratic Society (SDS). Although three people were killed by the blast, Kathy Boudin and a companion managed to escape and swiftly disappear into the underground. Eleven years later Kathy Boudin was captured by the police at a roadblock in Rockland County, New York, following an abortive armored car robbery in nearby Nanuet, which had resulted in the shooting deaths of a Brinks guard and two police officers. She eventually pleaded guilty in 1984 to reduced charges and was given a sentence of twenty years to life, which she is currently serving.

Because political radicals were involved in the crimes, there was such immediate and strong hostility against Boudin in Rockland County that her trial was twice moved to other counties before her guilty plea was made and accepted. During the initial steps of her pretrial incarceration, she was treated so horribly that a federal judge was forced to issue an order condemning her captors for their conduct. However, to nullify his decision, she was moved out of his jurisdiction just before he issued it. After almost two years of such draconian treatment, the authorities finally relented and began to treat her as any other pretrial detainee.

I have known Kathy for more than twenty years and have the greatest respect for her. Like so many young people in the sixties, she saw her country engaged in wanton brutality at home and abroad, much of it generated by what one American President once referred to as "the springs of racial poison." She worked in economically depressed ghettos and saw, at first hand, the misery and desperation that combined to destroy human beings who, by the sheer accident of birth, were born black. It is hardly surprising that she reacted so strongly to the evils she saw everywhere around her.

There are many who have harshly criticized her for being part of the ill-fated Rockland County venture. There are still others who pilloried her for opting for a conventional legal approach to the resulting criminal charges rather than holding herself out as a prisoner of war and refusing to interpose any defense other than that the court lacked jurisdiction over her. Despite the deep hurt she must have felt over these conflicting yet equally denigrating opinions, she managed, under the most arduous of surroundings and treatment, to maintain her dignity and sense of self-worth. She can expect to spend most of the latter part of her life in prison but she will, if I know her, continue to try to improve the lot of those who are sharing her new environment with her.

Kathy Boudin

They treated her with hatred from the start
    By plotting out a medieval plan
Designed to break her spirit and her heart
    And punish her before her trial began.
They moved her secretly from jail to jail
    In violation of the law's command;
They hammered in each denigrating nail
    And would not let her baby touch her hand.
Whenever she was taken from her cell,
    A mass of police patrolled the courthouse mall
So that prospective jurors could foretell
    That they might judge a danger to them all.
The system has its methods to lash out
    At those who hold its principles in doubt.

The Prosecutors

What the law calls prosecutorial misconduct has reached such endemic proportions that a high-ranking federal appellate judge was recently moved to condemn what he termed "flagrant abuse of professional standards . . . [by] . . . competitive and ambitious prosecutors [who] think that to win by any means is the 'name of the game'." The tactics employed by these worthies have included suppressing evidence favorable to a defendant or fabricating that which points the finger at him or her, inflammatory summations, deliberately incomplete investigations, prejudicial leaks to the news media, and hidden deals with key witnesses. One went so far, in a rape-murder death penalty case, as to dip the defendant's undershorts in red paint and have a chemist perjure himself that they were stained with blood of the victim's type.

However, no matter how egregious the official misconduct, no one guilty of it has, to my mind, ever been prosecuted. One New Jersey intermediate appellate court recently bemoaned the fact that "[w]e cannot be sure that stern warnings and occasional reversals have been sufficient to control the problem. It may be time for our Supreme Court to consider disciplinary proceedings as a means of holding this conduct in check." Despite these brave words, however, the judges simply cannot bring themselves to punish errant prosecutors adequately, a reluctance that is sure to encourage more "competitive and ambitious prosecutors. . . ."

The Prosecutors

They suborn perjury without a thought,
    Convinced that they are on the side of right;
Their crucial witnesses are sold and bought
    By promises that never see the light.
They pass off paint as blood the victim shed,
    And hide confessions of another man;
They hesitate to follow any thread
    That might cast doubt upon their master plan.
They leak misleading data to the press
    Designed to prejudice their quarry's flight,
And if his race is black they do their best
    To see to it his jury is all-white.
They feel secure, no matter what they do,
    That they will never be indicted, too.

Angela Y. Davis

In 1970, sixteen-year-old Jonathan P. Jackson, whose brother George was a well-known black revolutionary serving a sentence of one-to-life in California's San Quentin Prison, tried to free him by kidnapping a Marin County Superior Court judge and holding him until his brother was released. After the judge was taken at gunpoint from the courthouse, the authorities opened fire, and in the ensuing shootout, both Jackson and his hostage were killed. Later, Angela Y. Davis, a black woman and a Communist, who had openly purchased the guns used by Jackson, her former bodyguard, was indicted for the judge's abduction and murder.

As a member of the faculty of a state university, Davis had long been a target of numerous unsuccessful attempts to discharge her because of her political views. She was held without bail for almost two years, until the abolition of the death penalty in California, when she was finally granted bond and released. Her trial before an all-Caucasian jury in September of 1972 finally resulted in her acquittal, and the sonnet's last couplet contains her almost verbatim answer to a reporter's postverdict query as to whether she had received a fair trial. Although I did not represent her, I visited her before her release on bail in her two-room cell at the ultramodern Marin County Jail.

Angela Davis

A black, a woman and a Communist,
    She dared to raise her voice above the rest,
Until her name appeared on every list
    Designed to isolate each vocal pest.
At first they tried to prove she was unfit,
    Like Socrates, to teach our tender youth,
That opposition to official writ
    Made her incapable of seeing truth.
When that all failed, she was accused of crime,
    Charged with the causing of a fatal spree,
And kept in jail for much too long a time
    Until an all-white jury set her free.
"The fairest trial," she told the press's call,
    "Would certainly have been no trial at all."

Hanging Judge

Throughout my career I have appeared before many "hanging judges" in all parts of the country. I was tempted to name some of my candidates for this designation, but after some reflection I decided not to do so for fear of being involved in libel suits galore. However, I am sure that most of those I could have named know their own passions and prejudices well enough to realize that I was thinking of them when I wrote this sonnet.

One of the pressing problems with the selection of judges, whether by appointment or election, is that former prosecutors are so often elevated to both the federal and state benches. I once did some research on the background of the members of the United States District Court for the Southern District of New York and discovered that a substantial majority had formerly been prosecutors. The same is apparently true for state judges throughout the nation.

The trouble with this type of judicial selection is that those used to prosecuting criminal defendants are suddenly thrust into far different roles in which they must surmount their previous leanings and become impartial arbiters, a metamorphosis, I believe, that is almost an impossible one. In addition, these judges are daily confronted by members of their old offices who appear before them, a situation that would tax the impartiality of a Solomon.

As I understand the British system, there are no professional prosecutorial agencies in serious criminal cases, and members of the defense bar are selected at random to represent the Crown in such matters. It is my deep feeling that the practice of making the District Attorney's office a routine stepping stone to judicial office should cease and some other method of selection adopted to name our judges. However, I also know that the system uses the criminal law to maintain the status quo and that it will continue to see to it that, wherever possible, former prosecutors occupy the seats of judgment.

Hanging Judge

For him the question is how to proceed
    To make the Constitution seem supreme,
Yet give the prosecutors what they need
    In order to achieve their fondest dream.
By utilizing different vocal tones
    Or grimaces that show his preference,
He lets the jurors know whose ax he hones
    And how they should consider evidence.
He frames his charge in language that is meant
    To ascertain the panel does not stray;
He sees to it that precedent is bent
    If it can safely be explained away.
A lynching mob of one, he knows
    That he can hide behind judicial clothes.

Bar Examination

After surviving law school, would-be attorneys have one final hurdle to clear—the bar examination. In New York this two-day marathon, designed to test applicants in all aspects of the law, is given in huge, drafty, and often bleak halls. The arduousness of the examination, coupled with the eagerness of its takers to pass it, has spawned a pedagogical phenomenon known as bar review courses which, for a fancy fee, will force feed their anxious clients with the requisite knack and knowledge.

In any event there are many, including myself, who feel that the only proper way to prepare graduates for the practice of law is not by testing their abilities to regurgitate memorized principles, but by requiring a suitable apprentice period. The profession is so filled with functional incompetents, particularly in the trial arenas, that something more than just another written test is needed to weed them out. Recently, the Supreme Court, recognizing this sorry state of affairs, was forced to alter the standard for judging incompetence of counsel in order to make it easier for victimized clients to obtain suitable redress.

Bar Examination

Three years of endless courses finally through,
    The time has come at least to prove to all
That one has mastered all the law that's due
    And safely may accept the public's call.
The mammoth testing hall is filled with those
    Whose minds are crammed with contracts, torts, and
    sales,
As proctors wander up and down the rows,
    Alert to see that honesty prevails.
The only sounds that permeate the air
    Are several thousand pages being turned
As would-be lawyers demonstrate their flair
    For understanding all that they have learned.
There is no wait that's longer than the one
    Before the right to practice law is won.

The Rosenbergs

The tragedy of Julius and Ethel Rosenberg has been so extensively documented that it hardly needs much more elaboration. Suffice it to say, they were convicted in 1951, along with electrical engineer Morton Sobell, of conspiring in the mid-forties to give the secret of the atom bomb to the Soviet Union. Sentenced to death, on Friday, June 19, 1953, the Rosenbergs were electrocuted at Sing Sing Prison in Ossining, New York, just before the beginning of the Jewish Sabbath. Their case attracted worldwide attention with most foreign observers regarding them as Cold War martyrs.

In the United States, on the other hand, the nature of the charges against them thoroughly terrified the liberal community. The American Civil Liberties Union, for one, not only saw no civil liberties issues raised by their trial but denied that there was anything unconstitutional about the death sentences imposed upon them. The American Jewish Committee took much the same position and even went so far as to oppose the granting of executive clemency to the couple. The desertion of the Rosenbergs by all but their most ardent supporters is graphic evidence that fear is sometimes stronger than resolve, and for most of us self-preservation can easily subvert our highest principles.

Hours before their scheduled execution, Circuit Judge Jerome Frank, a Jew and a civil libertarian, refused to join a willing conservative colleague and grant a stay for further argument on a substantial point of law; namely, whether capital punishment was applicable if, at the time of the alleged offense, the United States was not officially at war. The three lawyers—Arthur Kinoy, Marshall Perlin, and Samuel Gruber—who had rushed to Frank's home in New Haven, Connecticut, were shocked when he refused to agree to the stay. Frank said, "If I were as young as you are, I would be sitting where you are now and saying and arguing what you are arguing. You are right to do so, but when you are as old as I am, you will understand why I cannot do what you ask. I cannot do it."

The Rosenbergs

Waves of hysteria had swept the land,
      Whipped by the demagogue's most telling lies;
The paralyzing fear was daily fanned
      That we were threatened by a host of spies.
The Russians had the bomb, they let us see,
      A fact we simply never had believed
They could, without the aid of thievery,
      Have ever scientifically achieved.
We seized upon this sacrificial pair
      To bring about the saving of our face,
And did what could be done to blight their prayer
      For justice in the legal marketplace.
To show the world our understanding heart,
      We took their lives before the Sabbath's start.

Bertrand Russell

I never met Lord Bertrand Russell, the world-renowned British philosopher and mathematician, who was awarded the 1950 Nobel Prize for Literature, and I was surprised, to put it mildly, to receive a trans-Atlantic telephone call from him in 1969. A confirmed pacifist who organized demonstrations against nuclear weapons and the Vietnam war, he informed me that a major American munitions firm had used a sketch of him without his permission or knowledge in a Help Wanted advertisement in the *New York Times*. To add insult to injury, the caption under the sketch indicated that he had died some years ago. I contacted the company in question and arranged for a cash settlement to be paid to Russell's Stockholm Peace Conference. After I had sent the money to the client, Russell invited me to be his guest at the upcoming conference. Unfortunately, he died just before it began.

Bertrand Russell

A man of peace, he won the funded prize
    Created from the sales of dynamite,
And spoke against the ignorance of lies
    That threatened to expand the darkest night.
The war in Vietnam incurred his wrath
    As did the specter of an atom blast,
He sought to put his world upon the path
    Where love was free and armies were not massed.
His life was long but far from long enough
    To reach his heartfelt universal goal
When we could choose the soft hand for the rough
    With freedom from a radiated hole.
Of all his complicated formulae,
    The most enduring was—we shall not die!

Grenada

I met Prime Minister Maurice Bishop of Grenada in August, 1983, when he spoke at New York's Hunter College. We had a pleasant backstage talk, and he invited me to visit his country on the fifth anniversary of the overthrow of the erratic government of Prime Minister Eric M. Gairy, who had turned to astrology for the answers to all of the island's problems. Two months after our meeting Bishop was shot to death during a "power struggle" in his New Jewel Party, and on October 25, 1983, the United States took immediate advantage of the momentary chaos caused by the tragedy to invade Grenada and put an end to the island's brief experiment in socialism. The pretext used by the President of the United States was the need to protect several hundred American students at St. George's University School of Medicine. In the explanation given to the Marines involved in Operation Urgent Fury, its code name, the purpose of the invasion was to liberate Grenada from its Marxist government and expel the Cubans who were building the jet airport. Bishop had hoped that a new airport would make the tourist trade as significant to Grenada's economy as its fabled nutmeg crop.

My anger at the invasion led me to create a parody on Francis Scott Key's *Star Spangled Banner*. Recalling that lawyer Key had written his familiar words while held captive on a British warship during the shelling of Baltimore's Fort McHenry in 1814, I tried to imagine what he might have composed had he been on the deck of an American destroyer involved in Urgent Fury. His new version could easily have been:

> Oh, say, can we seize by the dawn's early light
> Where so grossly we sailed at the President's scheming?
> Whose broad hypes and trite slurs, through the unequal fight,
> Ó'er airwaves he controlled were so recklessly streaming,
> And the rocket's red glare, the bombs bursting in air,
> Gave proof to the right that its precepts we share.
> Oh, say, does that greed-strangled banner yet wave
> O'er the land of the few and the home of their knave.

Grenada

Grenada has less souls than four blocks square
    In New York City or Los Angeles;
Her people earn their meager daily fare
    From touring visitors or nutmeg trees.
The White House said it was the time to meet
    The threat to national security
Posed by its tiny socialist retreat
    Among the islands of the southern sea.
The pretext was an internecine fight
    That ripped the New Jewel leadership apart;
Marines destroyed the four-year flickering light
    That had been growing stronger since its start.
Our President, it seems, is never loathe
    To call upon the hypocritic oath.

Maurice Bishop

This lawyer, trained in Britain's ancient ways,
    Came home to oust a lunatic from power,
And turned his country from its star-struck craze
    Toward socialism's most redeeming hour.
With poverty an ever-present sore,
    Enough to challenge any Marxist state,
He welcomed tourists to his island shore
    Provided they could pay the going rate.
But first there had to be a new airport
    With runways long enough for every jet;
When Cuba sent logistical support,
    The waves from Washington broke higher yet.
One hopes his dying eyes could not foresee
    That cruel October end to sovereignty.

Morris L. Ernst

Morris L. Ernst was always one of my heroes. He and my father had been childhood friends, and he was constantly described to me by my parents as a good man and a great lawyer. I can still remember when he won the landmark decision that exonerated James Joyce's *Ulysses* from charges of obscenity. When I was in law school, I used to visit him at his office for advice, and secretly I hoped to be invited to join his firm where one of my cousins was already an associate. After I opened my own office, I took many of my problems to him, and I was flattered beyond words when he included one of those visits in his published diary.

As general counsel to the American Civil Liberties Union, with which I have been associated in one capacity or another for more than thirty years, he was one of the guiding lights of that organization and a role model for attorneys like me. After his death in 1976, it was revealed, through the Freedom of Information Act, that for almost three decades he had been writing "Dear Edgar" letters to FBI Director Hoover in which he furnished information about both the Union's internal activities and those of many of its members. In addition, he had proposed to Hoover in 1952, that if the Bureau approved, he would try to infiltrate the Rosenberg defense team in order to persuade the couple to confess. If Julius Rosenberg "breaks and tells all he knows," Ernst told Hoover, "this would be a terrific story and probably would be most helpful to the Bureau." Even Hoover seemed appalled at such an unprincipled suggestion.

Recently, in a *Nation* article about the Hoover-Ernst correspondence, former *New York Times* correspondent Harrison E. Salisbury put the strange relationship of these two men in proper perspective. "A profound lesson can be drawn from the letters, particularly at this time when, again, those manning the ramparts of civil liberties are pondering the consequences of close association between the defenders of free expression and those who seek to undermine and violate its foundations in our democracy."

Morris L. Ernst

He was my father's friend, so long ago,
    And in my house his name was often heard,
It was my hope that I would get to know
    The same delight that sparked his every word.
While I was still a student at the Bar,
    I sat beside his desk, year after year,
This man who was my legal shining star,
    The model who would shape my own career.
He taught me that the Constitution stands
    Between the tyrant and democracy,
That only work of many willing hands
    Could keep our country relatively free.
I'm glad I didn't' know he was a spy
    For his "Dear Edgar" Hoover's FBI.

Freedom of the Press

This sonnet was based, in part, upon a remark attributed to the late Indian Prime Minister Jawaharlal Pandit Nehru upon the occasion of his visit to the United States in the early sixties. When a reporter asked him what he thought about America's vaunted freedom of the press, he is supposed to have replied, " As I understand it, it means that anyone who is rich enough to own a newspaper can print whatever he pleases."

Freedom of the Press

The First Amendment means that only those
    With cash enough to own a printing press
Could circulate whatever news they chose
    And withhold what they wanted to suppress.
They tell us whom to fear and love and hate
    And how to cogitate about it all;
Their products are too often purloined straight
    From handouts that the government lets fall.
They dramatize the trivia of life,
    Ignoring what they do not comprehend,
And thrive on murder, suicide, and strife
    As long as circulation's on the mend.
The only way to guess what's false or true
    Is read between the lines with derring-do.

The Surrender of Dennis Banks

On February 6, 1973, a demonstration by members of the Amer-
ican Indian Movement in Custer, South Dakota—sparked by the
fatal stabbing of a young Indian by a white man—degenerated
into a physical confrontation between the protesters and police
officers. As a result, Dennis Banks and a group of Native Ameri-
cans were charged with a number of crimes. Three weeks later
Banks was one of the leaders of the occupation of the hamlet of
Wounded Knee, for which he was forced to stand trial in St. Paul,
Minnesota, during most of 1974. After these charges were ulti-
mately dismissed because of pervasive governmental misconduct,
he returned to Custer, where he was convicted of assault and riot
charges against him in 1975. Before he could be sentenced, how-
ever, he fled the state and eventually sought sanctuary in Califor-
nia because of fear that his life would be in danger if he were
incarcerated in South Dakota.

After a lengthy investigation, and the receipt of a petition con-
taining 1,400,000 signatures in Banks's favor, then Governor
Edmund G. Brown, Jr. refused to extradite him and he began a
highly productive life on the West Coast. In addition to attending
college, he became first the vice-president and then the chancel-
lor of D-Q University, an Indian-Chicano adjunct of the California
higher education system.

After the 1982 election of Brown's successor, George Deuk-
mejian, who had made a campaign promise to extradite Banks if
he became governor, the AIM leader and his family moved to the
Onondaga Reservation near Syracuse, New York. He remained
there until September of 1984 when he decided to surrender to
South Dakota authorities and end his fugitive status. On Septem-
ber 13, he turned himself in to the Sheriff of Custer County for
sentencing by the judge who had tried his case. I wrote this son-
net as I was waiting for the latter to mount the bench for a hear-
ing which resulted in denial of bail.

On October 8, one of the most remarkable sentencing hear-
ings that I have ever attended took place in the Custer County
Courthouse. More than two dozen witnesses—including elders
from the Onondaga and Pine Ridge Reservations, a university

president, artists, writers, attorneys, AIM leaders, church personnel, ex-students, and former associates—spoke on Dennis's behalf. He was described by one as a "model for Indian people," and by another as "one of those rare individuals, indispensable and irreplaceable." Russell Means, his coleader at Wounded Knee, who had himself been convicted in Custer, told the judge that it was time "for a reconciliation between white and red in South Dakota."

Banks then asked permission to address the court. In a forty-five-minute narrative, during which he stood before the bench and spoke to the judge "as one human being to another," he detailed his life from his birth in Minnesota to his surrender. It was impossible for anyone not to be moved by his remarks, and the judge was visibly affected by what he was hearing. Many spectators in the tiny courtroom were holding back tears as Dennis turned to them and urged that no matter what happened to him they must continue the struggle for the rights of Native Americans to live in peace and dignity on the land they once owned as sovereign peoples.

With obvious reluctance the judge imposed a sentence of three years. Even though we felt that any sentence in his case was wholly unjustified, we were relieved to hear that his sentence was less harsh than what we had expected. We agreed with one of the witnesses who had implored the judge,"We hope that he will soon be set free so that he can continue to do his work for all of humankind."

The Surrender of Dennis Banks

I sit in court beside my longtime friend
    And wait for the proceeding to begin,
With nothing but my memories to defend,
    Where visions of the past can wander in.
The judge arrives, as regular as mail,
    And knows exactly what he means to do,
But listens to my prayer for lowered bail
    As if my pleading would be followed through.
The prosecutor knows that the die is cast
    And that it doesn't matter what he'll say
So long as he lets loose a strident blast
    To claim the state is fair in every way.
At last my friend goes through the alien door,
    Another warrior in chains once more.

Protest March

This sonnet represents a southern collage of protest marches that I witnessed during the sixties in such places as Birmingham and Selma, Alabama; Danville, Virginia; Albany, Georgia; and St. Augustine, Florida. What impressed me most about them was the dignity and courage of the marchers and the vicious brutality of the authorities. I believe that the sight of these confrontations on television screens around the country did more to enlist national support for the goals of these demonstrations than all the outraged specches and articles generated by them.

Protest March

The demonstrators marched on down the block,
    Their picket signs held high for all to see,
Demanding that the mayor advance the clock
    And grant to them their full equality.
They reached the forward line of waiting police
    And sank to earth upon each bended knee,
To pray that everlasting racial peace
    Would end the vestiges of slavery.
The billy clubs began to rise and fall
    While fire hoses washed the blood away;
The paddy wagons parked behind the wall
    And waited patiently for human prey.
The cameras rolled to catch the awful sight
    In time to make the evening news that night.

The Fountain Valley Five

The Virgin Islands, some one hundred in all, are part of the
Lesser Antilles chain. Discovered by Columbus in 1493, they be-
came, some 200 years later, the largest slave trading center in the
world. Denmark, which had bought the island of St. Croix from
France a century or so earlier, in 1848, was forced to abolish hu-
man bondage there when rebellious slaves kidnapped and held its
Royal Governor-General hostage. However, the freed Blacks con-
tinued, at starvation wages and under frightful working condi-
tions, to serve as the labor force for the operation of the many
cone-shaped sugar mills that dotted the landscape. Near each
press an ax was provided to hack off a worker's hands if they were
accidentally caught in the machinery so that the sugar extraction
process would not have to be stopped. Many of these edifices were
burnt to the ground in 1878 by the employees of the mills as a
protest against such intolerable treatment.

In order to protect the newly opened Panama Canal, the
United States bought St. Croix, St. Thomas, and St. John, three
of the largest islands in 1917 from the Danes for $25,000,000.
Because of their balmy climate, Old World atmosphere, and beau-
tiful beaches, the new possessions became a mecca for American
tourists. In addition, many stateside entrepreneurs purchased or
leased land on St. Croix, the reputed birthplace of Alexander
Hamilton, for commercial purposes. For example, Laurance S.
Rockefeller acquired an enormous tract in the center of the island
where he constructed a magnificent golf course known as Foun-
tain Valley, and introduced a unique breed of European beef
cattle, bred to survive with virtually no human assistance on the
area's rugged mountain terrain.

In September, 1972, eight people, including guests and golf
course personnel, were killed by gunfire at Fountain Valley. Five
young Crusans were charged with the murders and ultimately
convicted primarily on the strength of their alleged confessions.
However, one of the police officers involved in their interrogation
admitted that they had been tortured by electric cattle prods ap-
plied to their genitalia as well as by hangings, beatings, and near
drownings in a toilet bowl. A massive FBI investigation produced

substantial evidence that such brutalities had indeed taken place. Despite these revelations the trial judge refused to suppress the confessions in question, and after nine days of jury deliberations the five men were found guilty and are currently serving eight consecutive life terms.

I represented Beaumont Gereau, one of the Fountain Valley defendants. At the time of his arrest Gereau told his captors that "they took our basketball away," which meant that the island, which was 80 percent black, was totally dominated by its white minority.

On the last day of 1984, Ishmael Ali LaBeet, another defendant, hijacked a plane on which he was being transported from the Virgin Islands to the United States, following a court appearance. He forced it to land in Havana, where he was taken into custody by the local police. Since it has been Cuban policy not to return airplane hijackers to the United States, he will, given his political background, probably not be extradited from that country.

The Fountain Valley Five

The island calls itself the best on earth
    For sun and bays and sand and gentle waves,
The site of Hamilton's reputed birth
    And where they lopped off hands of careless slaves.
The Crusans forced, by threatening to kill
    Their Governor, the Danes to set them free,
And later torched each hated sugar mill,
    The symbols of their neoslavery.
Today the Rockefellers run the show
    And graze their cattle on an awesome spread,
While blacks live out their lives on shanty row
    And wait on tourists for their daily bread.
One of the five suspects was heard to say,
    "Hey, man, they took our basketball away!"

Richard M. Boardman

In the late sixties I represented Rick Boardman, a member of a strong Quaker family, who had applied for and received conscientious objector status from the draft. As a conscientious objector he was required by the Selective Service System to perform the alternative service, namely, to work in a hospital. Because he refused the alternative service, he was indicted for draft evasion and tried in a Boston federal court before the same octogenarian judge who had presided at the celebrated trial, a few years earlier, of Dr. Benjamin Spock and others for conspiring to persuade eligible youths to avoid military service. Because he was white and a Quaker, Rick's defense was that he was being given a preferential status denied to blacks, who could not submit the required extensive documentation of a long history of religious pacifism so easily produced by Quakers. This was one inspirational example of a young pacifist who went to jail rather than take advantage of a privilege available to whites only. I can't think of anyone I was prouder to represent than this man for any and all seasons.

United States v. Richard M. Boardman

His Quaker background gave him ready claim
    To strong religious scruples toward the war,
So he submitted forms to have his name
    Approved as one opposed to blood and gore.
Accepted as an honest pacifist,
    He was excused from military call
If he obeyed an order to enlist
    For two years' duty in a hospital.
He learned that blacks who could not prove their creed,
    No matter how sincere their moral stand,
Were being sent in droves to fight and bleed
    In some unhappy southeast Asian land.
He thought it time for good Friends to rebel
    And yielded privilege for a prison cell.

Itinerant Lawyers

Long before the American colonies became a nation, the nonresident lawyer had become a hallmark of the legal profession. When John Peter Zenger, the New York printer accused of seditious libel for publicly criticizing the provincial governor, found his local attorneys disbarred for daring to represent him, he obtained the services of Andrew Hamilton of Philadelphia, who succeeded in winning an acquittal for his new client. Throughout the years that followed this celebrated case, many American lawyers have responded to similar calls for aid. California's Frederick H. Moore, who appeared for Nicolo Sacco and Bartolomeo Vanzetti in their 1921 trial for the murder in Dedham, Massachusetts—surely one of the most controversial cases of this or any other century—is another unforgettable example.

Unfortunately, the United States Supreme Court, in 1979, decided that state courts had the arbitrary right to prevent nonresident counsel from practicing before them. In a momentous dissent, Justice Stevens, joined by Justices Marshall and Brennan, quoted the words of a lower court judge who well understood the value to society at large of the traveling lawyer:

Nonresident lawyers have appeared in many of our most celebrated cases. For example, Andrew Hamilton, a leader of the Philadelphia bar, defended John Peter Zenger in New York in 1735 in colonial America's most famous freedom-of-speech case. Clarence Darrow appeared in many states to plead the cause of an unpopular client, including the famous *Scopes* trial in Tennessee where he opposed another well-known, out-of-state lawyer, William Jennings Bryan. Great lawyers from Alexander Hamilton and Daniel Webster to Charles Evans Hughes and John W. Davis were specially admitted for the trial of important cases in other states. A small group of lawyers appearing *pro hac vice* inspired and initiated the civil rights movement in its early stages. In a series of cases brought in courts throughout the South, out-of-state lawyers Thurgood Marshall, Constance Motley and Spottswood Robinson, before their appointments to the federal bench, developed the legal principles which gave rise to the civil rights movement.

There are a number of reasons for this tradition. The demands of

186

business and the mobility of our society are the reasons given by the American Bar Association in Canon 3 of the Code of Professional Responsibility. That canon discourages 'territorial limitations' on the practice of law, including trial practice. There are other reasons in addition to business reasons. A client may want a particular lawyer for a particular kind of case, and a lawyer may want to take the case because of the skill required. Often, as the case of Andrew Hamilton, Darrow, Bryan and Thurgood Marshall, a lawyer participates in a case out of a sense of justice. He may feel a sense of duty to defend an unpopular defendant and in this way to give expression to his own moral sense. These are important values, both for lawyers and clients, and should not be denied arbitrarily.

Fortunately, most state courts have freely admitted nonresident attorneys to practice before them, usually on a reciprocity basis. But the ability of a client to be represented by a lawyer of choice should not be a matter of judicial largesse. As one court put it, almost forty years ago, "To hold that defendants in a criminal trial may not be defended by the lawyers they want is to destroy the constitutional right to a fair trial."

Itinerant Lawyers

"Have writ, will travel" is their stock in trade,
    These learned nomads of the open road,
Who cross the boundaries of their states to aid
    Those persecuted by the legal code.
When Zenger's New York counsel were repressed,
    A Philadelphia lawyer took their place,
And Sacco and Vanzetti looked out west
    To find a champion for their murder case.
Throughout the South and then at Wounded Knee,
    The out-of-staters roamed from court to court,
To fight for those still held in slavery
    And Indians who were the white man's sport.
The law these men and women upheld well
    Wrought truth from lies and heaven out of hell.

Anonymous Jury

In 1977, for the first time in Anglo-American jurisprudence, a court granted the prosecution's request that the names of the jurors be withheld from the defense. Since that time, in a number of highly publicized cases, including the Los Angeles trial of John DeLorean on cocaine charges, judges have entered similar orders. The result is that, in these cases, jurors are identified only by numbers, and are given further anonymity with respect to both their addresses and places of employment. The concept of the anonymous jury is, in the words of one law professor, "[a] devastating blow . . . to the presumption of innocence." Also condemning the practice, a federal appellate judge commented that it would "have far-reaching consequences that are harmful and injurious beyond measurement."

Be that as it may, it is extremely likely, given the present judicial climate, that similar juries will be impaneled in controversial cases whenever the prosecutor feels the need of an extra edge over the defense. In a society that now tolerates preventive detention, excessive bail, "cruel and unusual punishment" and illegal searches and seizures, the pragmatic philosophy that the end justifies the means is rapidly sweeping fundamental constitutional safeguards under the rug of our own fears and uncertainties.

Anonymous Jury

The prosecutors found a way that's new
    To guarantee convictions by the score,
By hiding jurors' names from public view
    And using numbers as descriptive lore.
The judge then tells the panel that they should hide
    The place where they may earn their daily bread
And not particularize where they reside,
    But give the section of the town instead.
Although they're told that anonymity
    Is meant to spare them from reporters' guile,
They do believe, in actuality,
    It's to protect them from the man on trial.
One lawyer whispers in his client's ear,
    "Does fifty-four a Jewish name appear?"

Greensboro

On November 3, 1979, while members and supporters of the militant Communist Workers Party (CWP) were assembling in Greensboro, North Carolina, to mount an anti-Klan demonstration, a number of vehicles, filled with members of the Ku Klux Klan and the American Nazi Party, drove into the area. Despite the presence of television cameras, which graphically filmed the event, the Klansmen and the Nazis stopped their cars and began to fire at carefully selected CPW leaders, fatally wounding five of them, four men and one woman. Despite the fact that a number of the killers were later charged with a variety of crimes in both state and federal indictments, they were all acquitted when they were able to persuade their susceptible juries that they had been reasonably provoked by their radical victims.

Although a federal undercover agent accompanied the killers and kept the authorities informed of their mood and arsenal, the Greensboro police stayed discreetly out of sight until the massacre was over.

The concept that some American lives have far less value than others is hardly confined to Greensboro. Just before this book went to press, the Philadelphia police, as an eviction aid, dropped a concussion bomb from a helicopter on a house occupied by members of MOVE, a small black back-to-nature group, who had angered their neighbors by their unorthodox life styles. The result—the incineration of seven adults and four children, and the destruction of almost sixty homes.

Greensboro

The radicals prepared to demonstrate
    Against the riders of the Ku Klux Klan,
Arriving at the place where they would wait
    Until they formed their protest caravan.
From out of town a line of cars drew near,
    Replete with murderous men and guns galore;
The city's police obligingly stayed clear
    Although they knew that violence was in store.
Self-styled as the United Racist Front,
    The Klansmen and the Nazis reached their goal,
And then began their ordained human hunt
    That left five broken bodies as its toll.
Two juries made it plain to everyone
    That Commie lives could safely be undone.

Margie Velma Barfield

In 1978, 45-year-old Margie Velma Barfield was sentenced to death by a Bladen County, North Carolina, jury for the fatal arsenic poisoning of her fiance, farmer Stuart Taylor. After her conviction she admitted she had similarly murdered her mother and two elderly people whom she cared for as a part-time nurse, John Henry Lee and Dollie Edward. After her appeals were exhausted, the trial judge set her execution for November 2, 1984, four days before the general election at which Democratic Governor James B. Hunt, Jr. was a candidate for the U.S. Senate against incumbent Jesse A. Helms. On September 27, 1984, Governor Hunt denied Barfield's petition for commutation of her sentence. In doing so, he pointed out that 77 percent of the letters about the case received by his office from North Carolinians approved of her death sentence.

Because of my aversion to capital punishment, I contacted James D. Little and Richard H. Burr, who were Barfield's attorneys, and volunteered the services and resources of the Center for Constitutional Rights, a New York-based, nonprofit, educational and legal foundation of which I am vice-president. When my offer was accepted, the Center's cooperating attorney, Ronald L. Kuby, working with Little and Burr, prepared a last-minute appeal to both state and federal courts in North Carolina for a stay of execution. We hoped we would be given enough time in which to assemble and present evidence that Barfield was incompetent during the pretrial period because of her withdrawal from the large quantity of drugs she had been taking before her arrest.

Unfortunately, our efforts failed and, at 2 A.M. on November 2, 1984, she was put to death by an injection of lethal drugs, the first woman to be executed in the United States in more than a generation. As the hour of her death approached, demonstrators outside the prison cheered and applauded, leading the *New York Times* to observe that "the United States has taken a big step backward into barbarism." Ironically, Governor Hunt was soundly defeated by Senator Helms four days later.

In the early days of the English Common Law, mules and horses which kicked their masters to death were executed. Such acts were, in my opinion, as rational as taking the life of a woman who, while not legally insane when she poisoned her victims, was so emotionally disturbed as to make a death sentence wholly inappropriate. The only justification usually advanced by advocates of capital punishment is that it serves the dual goals of punishment and deterrence. In Margie Velma Barfield's case neither was attained.

Velma Barfield

They said she'd poisoned many fellow souls,
　　This wild-eyed nurse, a lunatic for sure,
And that, according to the statewide polls,
　　She had to die so others would stay pure.
The courts had passed upon her lawyers' plea,
　　And turned a deaf ear to their urgent words,
Deciding that her trial was fair and she
　　Deserved her fate, this woman mad as birds.
A judge had set her date with death to fall,
　　Just prior to the next Election Day,
So commutation would be hard to call,
　　If politics were there to block the way.
To make sure he won his Senate race,
　　The Governor withheld his saving grace.

Daddy King

On November 11, 1984, at the age of eighty-four, Martin Luther King's father died in Atlanta, Georgia, where for almost a half century he had pastored at the Ebenezer Baptist Church. The son of a cotton sharecropper in nearby Stockbridge, he had moved to Atlanta when he was sixteen years old, and he finally succeeded in fulfilling an adolescent ambition to become a preacher. Despite his solid middle class achievements, his life was deeply scarred by the assassination of one son, the drowning death of another, and the murder of his wife during Sunday worship.

I attended a number of Martin Luther King's sermons at Ebenezer during the sixties, and I well remember Daddy King, as he was known to all. When he listened to his illustrious son preach, he would frequently be moved to rap the dais platform with his cane and shout, "Martin, make it plain!" or similar exhortations. After services we would all repair to the church basement where a sumptuous dinner would be served. On these occasions Daddy King would hold court while Martin remained discreetly in the background. I was never quite sure that the elder King approved of all of Martin's positions, but I was certain that he had nothing but the deepest respect for the son who had made his name known throughout the world.

Daddy King

He lived beyond the tragedies that sent
   His wife and sons into the atmosphere;
He saw, within the span of his lament,
   The deadly signs of yesterday appear.
From Georgia's cotton fields he made his way
   To where a ready pulpit could be manned,
And taught his congregation how to pray
   For its deliverance from the master's hand.
Each Sunday morning, he'd exhort his sheep
   To keep the flag of tolerance unfurled,
Content to give his views a narrow sweep
   And leave it to his son to reach the world.
He'd bang the dais with his massive cane,
   And often shout, "Martin, make it plain!"

Roy M. Cohn

Roy Cohn was in my law school class, but I have little memory of him except that he was younger than the rest of us and sported a Bob Hope nose and slicked-down hair. Several years after graduation, he turned up as a member of the Rosenbergs's prosecution staff and, despite his age, played a prominent role in the successful effort to convict and execute the defendants. His work in that case so impressed Joseph R. McCarthy, the junior senator from Wisconsin who chaired the Permanent Subcommittee on Investigations, that Cohn became its chief counsel. Together with his youthful sidekick, G. David Schine, he became the scourge of many of McCarthy's targets, most of whom were scurrilously treated by the senator in his frenzied attempts to prove that communists permeated, among other agencies, the State Department and the Army.

McCarthy's indecent recklessness, aided and abetted by Cohn, was so gross that he was censured by the Senate in December, 1954, and immediately experienced a precipitous decline in his popularity and power. The censure vote took place after the televised Army-McCarthy hearings had exposed the Wisconsin legislator as an unprincipled, dangerous, and possibly demented, demagogue. However, in a nation of people who, in *New York Times* columnist James Reston's words, "have no memories," Cohn has not only survived his McCarthy period, but has become one of the country's most sought-after attorneys, despite the fact that he has since been federally indicted on a number of occasions for commercial crimes. Perhaps his subsequent acquittals were his best advertisements.

Roy Cohn

He did McCarthy's bidding night and day
  And hunted witches with a savage flair,
Until the Senate finally curbed the sway
  Of Gunner Joseph and his youthful pair.
Short years before, when barely out of school,
  He joined the prosecution's evil team
And then became its all too willing tool
  In efforts to achieve its nightmare dream.
But when the shoe was on the other limb
  And those he served so well charged him with crime,
He claimed his government had turned on him
  Because it did not like his upward climb.
Chameleons have their place in nature's plan
  But can the same be said of errant man?

John Fitzgerald Kennedy

John F. Kennedy's presidency has often been likened to Camelot, the legendary seat of King Arthur's chivalrous domain of high-minded, crusading knights of the egalitarian Round Table. However, as more and more facts begin to emerge about Kennedy and his administration, it has become quite clear that Camelot was a woeful misnomer. In this sonnet I have treated three aspects of the Kennedy years which, I am sure, King Arthur would have deplored.

The first is Kennedy's violation of the 1954 Geneva Accord that no country would station more than a limited number of military observers in Vietnam. In November, 1962, the President ordered 1,800 combat veterans into that country, the precursors of a force that would ultimately reach 500,000 troops. This decision marked the true beginning of the military involvement of the United States in Southeast Asia—a tragedy that was to result in the deaths of some 50,000 Americans and countless Vietnamese, the ravaging of that small country, and bitter, sometimes violent, divisions of opinion on the conflict here at home.

Second, although Kennedy campaigned vigorously on a strong civil rights plank in the Democratic platform, he did nothing to build upon it until Dr. King's demonstrations in the streets of Birmingham in the spring of 1963 forced his hand. In fact, his State of the Union message in January of that year did not ask Congress for any civil rights legislation. Faced with the nightly spectacle on national television of club-wielding police, fire hoses, and attack dogs dispersing King's supporters, the President was finally compelled to seek an appropriate antibias law, one which eventually became the Public Accommodations Act of 1964.

At that same time the administration was acutely aware that the FBI had opened what it termed "an intelligence investigation" of Dr. King. According to the late Frank Church's Senate Committee, which, in 1973–74, had conducted an in-depth analysis of the FBI's activities in this sphere, the White House knew that Attorney General Robert F. Kennedy had given FBI Director Hoover "written authorization to wiretap Dr. King and [his] offices," and that the FBI "was disseminating vicious characterizations of [him] within the Government," had "tape recordings embarrassing to [him] which it had offered to play to a White House official and to reporters," and had proposed "to 'leak' to reporters highly damaging accusations that some of [his] advisors were communists."

The Kennedy vendetta against Fidel Castro's Cuba has been so well documented that only brief references are here necessary. In April of 1961, the President approved a CIA project for a direct amphibious invasion of the island by anti-Castro refugees, an operation that took place on April 17, when 1,500 Cuban exiles stormed ashore at the *Bahia de Cochinos* (Bay of Pigs), some ninety miles south of Havana. The foray was crushed by Cuban armed forces within three days and, at the end of the year, the more than one thousand prisoners taken by Castro were exchanged for American food and medical supplies amounting to $52,000,000, all supposedly privately raised. After the Bay of Pigs fiasco, the administration negotiated with several Miami mobsters—all of whom were later mysteriously murdered—to assassinate Castro by such outlandish methods as poisoning his uniforms or his cigars.

John Fitzgerald Kennedy

He broke the international accord
    To put no combat troops in Vietnam,
And sent the first of the ensuing horde,
    A half a million sons of Uncle Sam.
He made no move to augment civil rights
    Until the streets of Birmingham ran red;
His wiretappers monitored the nights
    Of King so he could be discredited.
He tried to overthrow the Cuban state
    By underwriting an invasion's blows,
And, when it failed, he sought a hit man's rate
    To murder Castro with some poisoned clothes.
If this perverse regime was Camelot,
    The Holy Grail was just a chamber pot.

Fidel Castro

Over the years there have been many lawyers who were involved, in one degree or another, in revolutionary movements in their respective countries. Jefferson in America, Robespierre in France, Litvinov in Russia, and most recently, Bishop in Grenada—are notable examples of such practitioners. Today, perhaps the best known of such breed is Fidel Castro, the president of Cuba, who forced Fulgencia Batista, the man responsible for overthrowing that country's elected government in 1952, to flee for his life six years later.

Castro, who received his law degree from the University of Havana in 1950, initially sought to prevent Batista from seizing power by a court action charging him with treason. When this failed, he and a small band of followers, on July 26, 1953, attacked the Moncada military barracks in Santiago de Cuba. Although Castro and many of his supporters were captured in the unsuccessful operation, his speech made in his own defense at his trial several months later, known as "History Will Absolve Me," became his major political statement. Because of significant public pressure, Batista was forced to release him in 1955, and Castro then went to Mexico where, along with Che Guevara, he organized a group of Cuban exiles whom he trained in guerrilla tactics.

In late 1956, he and his tiny army returned to their homeland aboard the yacht *Granma*. After being severely mauled by Batista's waiting troops, Castro and his surviving companions managed to retreat into the Sierra Maestra mountain range in the southwestern Oriente Province from which they conducted a highly effective guerrilla campaign against Batista's army. Finally, on the last day of 1956, the dictator fled the country, and Castro's forces marched triumphantly into Havana and formed a new government for what their leader termed the "great family" of Cubans.

In September, 1960, Castro paid his second vist to New York since his assumption of power. After spending a night at one of the city's midtown luxury hotels, he suddenly decided to move to Harlem's Hotel Theresa. At the time I moderated an interview program on a New York radio station, and I rushed to the Theresa in hopes of taping the Cuban leader. Although I got to shake his hand and murmur a few well-rehearsed words in halting Spanish, there was just too much turmoil on his floor to make the necessary arrangements, and I left without my interview. I do remember that while I was waiting for the only operating elevator to take me to the lobby, someone asked me if I knew where Castro could obtain a freshly killed chicken. I referred my questioner to an area of Broadway, some twenty or so blocks to the south, where I remembered having seen a number of kosher butcher shops.

Fidel Castro

One year beyond Batista's grasp of power,
    This lawyer-leader started his campaign
To bring about a liberating hour
    And end the new regime's oppressive reign.
When the attack upon the barracks failed,
    He faced a trial before the tyrant's court,
Which decided that he must be jailed
    But soon was forced to cut his sentence short.
He left his land for Mexico and learned
    Just how a revolution must be led.
Until, with Che, he finally returned
    And saw Havana feel his army's tread.
He found that sometimes, when all talk is done,
    There's nothing more persuasive than a gun.